"Holy Mess provides helpful and necessary reminders for us all. Jesus freely gives Himself to us and desires for us to carry the Good News message of His grace to all the world. The miracle that He does that through messy and fickle people like ourselves isn't lost on me. He loves us and offers forgiveness and eternal hope to each who will call on Him. Thanks to Michelle for so eloquently putting words to the thoughts we have about our own lives that look so unworthy of such a Savior."
Amanda Bacon — Proverbs 31 Ministries, co-author of Shiny Things: Mothering on Purpose in a World of Distractions, co-host of All the Mom Things podcast

"Michelle beautifully displays the real, raw, mess-to-masterpiece story Jesus offers every single one of us in this heartfelt piece of art." **Kaitlin Chappell Rogers — author of "Not from God"**

"I'm a control freak. I like to have my hand in everything and feel like I have everything under my own control. But the truth is? I'm an absolute mess. It's always been a huge sigh of relief to open God's Word and read about other messes just like me (and you). Michelle's words in this book will welcome you in to say "you're not alone in your mess" but encourage you into the holiness that God has for you. You will feel a sigh of relief as she welcomes your mess to the table, shares her story and the stories of women of Scripture. With her gentle nudging and wise guidance, you'll find yourself more in love with the truth of the gospel and finding your mess turning into something beautiful." **Kara-Kae James — author of "Mom Up: Thriving with Grace in the Chaos of Motherhood"**

"Few books come along that touch us at our very core where our hurts, mistakes and failures hide, and shine the light of truth that God can use our brokenness for His glory and our good. Holy Mess encourages us to say yes to God and see what happens next." **Julie Kimmins — thrive! Ladies Ministry Director, Central Baptist Church Kannapolis, NC**

"Michelle invites you and me to the table no matter how messy our lives look. She tenderly walks us through several stories of women in the Bible that had some of the messiest lives. And through their stories she shows us what the power of the Gospel can do. It's a beautiful reminder to let God orchestrate His redemption no matter how impossible or messy life may seem. I know your heart will be encouraged and lifted through this genuine and Christ-centered book to live your best life even if it feels messy." **Micah Maddox — National Women's Conference Speaker and Author of Anchored In: Experience a Power-Full Life in a Problem-Filled World**

"If you are looking for a book that delivers rich wisdom gleaned from Scripture, practical advice, and encouragement that God can use even YOU, right where you are, then Holy Mess was written just for you! Michelle leads her readers on an excellent, in-depth study of several well-known women from the Bible while offering hope that not only is God not put off by our messiness, He can also use it for our good and His glory!" **Amy Hale - Bible teacher, speaker, and influencer showing women how to know God more personally through study of His Word**.

"Life is messy! And sometimes we need a friend to show us how the Scriptures help us push past the myth of perfection. Michelle Rabon is that friend. In Holy Mess, Michelle demystifies the illusion of perfection by weaving her personal life stories with similar stories from Scripture and leads us to cling to the presence of Christ and His perfect work in us." **Melissa Deming - Founder and creator of Heart and Hive**

"Holy Mess is a beautiful tribute to all women reminding us that even on the days we feel like the drivers of our very own Hot Mess Express, God will take the wheel and deliver us the kind of grace only He can provide. Rabon weaves powerful Scripture through her own relatable tales and continues to carry us right back to the foot of the cross - the place of hope and redemption. We don't have to measure up, strive or even barely survive - because we have God and in Him alone we can learn to thrive." **Erin Brown Hollis - Bestselling author of Cheers to the Diaper Years: 10 Truths for Thriving While Barely Surviving; and The Remarkable Housewives of the Bible Series; and Host of the Cheers To That! podcast.**

"For the woman who is yearning for both freedom and rest for her soul, Holy Mess will inspire you to release your emotional burdens and trust in the good news of the Gospel. Weaving Biblical stories with modern-day examples, Michelle tenderly walks you through real-life scenarios that threaten every woman's ability to live fully in God's grace and power. The end result as you arrive at the last page is a solid assurance of your worth in Jesus, a greater understanding of His desire and ability to restore your brokenness, and a hunger to trust Him with your future." **Heather M. Dixon, speaker and author of Determined: Living Like Jesus in Every Moment**

"Michelle's storytelling skills will hook you in each chapter of this study. She shows you how God's Word applies directly to you through the messy stories of Bible women and her own imperfect life. Her inspiration will help you dig deeper into the Bible with excitement to learn how God is speaking to you in your messes. You don't need to be perfect to do this study; just show up messy and feel refreshed." **Sarah Geringer - Author, blogger, speaker and artist at <u>sarahgeringer.com</u>**

"It isn't until we recognize the messes that we are that we obtain the grace we so desperately need. In Holy Mess, Michelle Rabon gives us the pass we need to admit our need and to breathe in the grace of God. She reveals how we so often try to control our messes rather than to trust God to use even our messes for His glory. Releasing control, the reader learns afresh how God can take our mess and use it to bless ourselves and others." **Denise Pass - Christian Artist, Author, Speaker and Worship Leader**

Holy Mess

WHAT IT MEANS TO BE A WOMAN
RADICALLY CHANGED BY THE GOSPEL

MICHELLE RABON
Displaying Grace

ISBN: 978-1-7330587-0-4

Interior and Cover Design: Michelle Rabon
www.holymessbook.com

~

**In loving memory of my Gran
and Lyndall.**
*These beautiful women changed
my life and taught me what
it means to truly love Jesus.*

~

Table of Contents

Dear Holy Mess Sister,

When I started writing this book, I imagined you and I would sit across from one another at the coffee shop having tea, or coffee, maybe even hot chocolate if that is your thing. We would laugh and cry as we shared our messes. Then we would wipe our running mascara and open God's Word together and find some hope for this *stuff* that we carry.

It is time for us to bring our mess to the table. The mess we lug with us; all the things we cannot let go of. All of it. Bring it to the table, the one that we share with the Father, the very place where the gospel meets us.

I never set out in life to write great words, much less a book. This book you hold in your hands was entirely directed by the works of God in my life. You see, the stories within these pages are ours. They don't just belong to the women of Scripture alone. We can see our faces in their stories, we weep with them, hurt with them, and rejoice in their triumphs through God's hand.

My prayer for this journey is that God will teach our hearts His truth, His power, and His love for us. This life we are traveling through together is challenging and overwhelming daily, but as His daughters, it is grace-filled every moment, grace straight from God. The gospel is powerful enough to have changed the lives of the women in this book. He is ready, waiting and eager to change ours too.

We try to mask our mess with phony perfection. We strive to be enough in a world that demands too much. But, there is relief from every hopeless burden. God desires to take your life and make it more than you could ever imagine. The Creator and Sustainer of the universe wants to gift you with a calling and an eternal future. It is a sweet offering that He is holding out to you today. Freedom.

This life can feel so warped and mangled by mess, the mess that sneaks up on us, and the mess that we create with our own hands. It can leave us reeling in a state of constant chaos. We muddle through our days hoping that one day we will have it all figured out, one day we will be better at this thing called life.

Consider this your stop sign.

At the intersection of mess and surrender, we see Jesus.

The One who desires to take our disastrous state and craft it into beauty, is the One who will cover our mess with His grace and mercy.

The messes we make require surrender, the messes we cannot control require grace, and the most magnificent mess of being changed and transformed by God requires a willing and repentant heart.

He takes what is broken and repairs it, and hauls the dirt of sin to the curb when we surrender our lives into His care. He doesn't leave us disorganized or broken down. He transforms us into holy daughters and refines our mess with His holiness and power. There is nothing we can do on our own to earn this gift. There are no works that will ever be enough to gain us favor with God and apart from salvation in Christ, we are without hope of escaping this mess we bear.

I have walked the road of discovering what it means to be a follower, gospel carrier, and a Holy Mess. God is faithful to meet us in it. Right here, right now. There is no mess that God cannot handle in His power. His love for you is so fierce it pursued death on your behalf. His mercy is so powerful, that even if it was only you, He would move heaven and earth to find and gain your heart. This truth will be evident through every page of this book. This truth is what drove women to repentance, it brought comfort in grief, forgiveness for mistakes, and power in weakness.

Write on these pages, mark them up with highlights, and notes. But more than that allow the truth of the gospel to change you and make you a Holy Mess.

Holy Mess - A woman transformed by the gospel. She isn't perfect, but she is redeemed and set apart with a Holy purpose.

INTRODUCTION

Let's Address the Mess

The sound of the impact was deafening, yet at that moment the impact seemed to bring my world to a frightening pause. One moment the laughter of my children filled the back seat as we discussed dinner plans and dance lessons. The next was as though the entire world went silent.

My gaze turned from the smiling faces in the rearview mirror to a slow-motion moment of terror. Out of the corner of my eye, I saw the car race toward us. The dusty red car came barreling through the stop sign; there was no time to react. Airbags exploded violently into my face as the car spun around. An eerie silence filled the air as we finally came to a stop. When I opened my eyes, smoke billowed from the front of my car, or what was left of it. Disoriented, I turned quickly to see my children shocked, but safe.

Strangers pulled us out and carried my children to safety. Sitting on the curb, all I could do was look at the wreckage in front of me - a car with a front end so crushed, it was as if it had never been there. People were rushing around us, a whirlwind of sirens, questions, and tears, yet to me, it was as if I was a ghost watching the commotion unfold in silence.

The hit to my head left me confused and unable to complete a sentence. My mind knew what it wanted to say, but my mouth was unable to form the words I needed. My husband pulled up to the scene not long after the accident and quickly tucked the children into his car out of sight as they loaded me onto the stretcher.

There was no escaping the tears as I rode in the ambulance. The numbness of shock was beginning to wear off, and in its place, searing pain from injuries and desperate panic from a wave of uncontrollable fear came over me. The chaos happening in my mind seemed to be enough to drown the rest of the world out. *How did this happen? How did she not see the stop sign? What if I had been a few seconds faster and my children would have taken the full brunt of the impact rather than me?* The accident could have quickly ripped everything away from me.

There is no preparation for moments like these, an instant epically etched into the hardwiring of our memories. One moment can quickly change the landscape of how we live our lives. These moments change us because God gives us the chance to live.

Even now, several years later, the accident still replays in my mind from time to time as if it were still fresh. It took months to recover from the severe concussion and broken tailbone. The deep blue and purple bruises that stared back at me in the mirror for weeks reminded me of how much worse it could have been. Each injury was a fiercely beautiful reminder of grace and mercy.

God can use life-altering moments to grab our attention and remind us we aren't where we need to be. When we aren't listening, He will allow life to pull us to attention.

In my season of recovery, God taught me hard truths. Things I had long believed about my faith and about who God was – was brought into the light.

Before the accident there was still so much I needed to learn, so much I had pushed aside for the sake of ease, and that included my walk with God. I had this idea in my head that perfection was required of me if I was to get this "faith" thing right.

The struggle wasn't because of God, it was because of me and my desire to be perfect, to be enough and mask all my scars from being seen. My faith-view had become about earning my standing with God rather than fully trusting the finished work of the cross.

Jesus did not take our sins to the cross for us to remain unchanged.

Even after giving my life to Christ many years before the accident, I believe it was in this season God showed me the truth of the gospel. He taught me that to Him my mess was worth the trouble. He pursued me in my brokenness out of pure love and desired to change me for His glory and my benefit. God can do amazing things with a woman in shambles if she surrenders it all.

Friend, our quest to prove our worth and show we have it all together is wearing us out.

I am tired.

Are you?

How did we get here? How did we get to a place where things have to be perfect for us to feel worthy? Where we need "likes" from strangers to feel approved of and accepted? We have let the world distort what we should be giving the gospel the final say over.

The gospel takes our mess from a total disaster that destroys us, to something holy that God intends to use. But, His grace is no license to keep making deliberate messes and no excuse to stay where we are. Will grace equal perfection for us? No, but it does allow us to live in the gospel truth of forgiveness and eternal hope through Jesus Christ.

Jesus did not take our sins to the cross for us to remain unchanged.

That Girl

I spent much of my life never wanting anything to do with God, mostly because I never thought He wanted anything to do with me. I never saw a girl good enough for Jesus when I looked in the mirror. Not to mention I couldn't wrap my mind around the possibility of who He might be or what He could want from me. Still, I believed the enemy who whispered, "God doesn't want what you bring to the table."

If we can get real for a second, most of us have heard the same whisper. We question our value in God's eyes and begin to believe we might be too much of a blemished case for Him to handle.

I believed what the enemy fed me. Have you? He has made us question our value and worth in the eyes of the One who created us. Satan's cunning attempts made me fail to see the massive need lingering within my soul. The lies that became woven around my heart became my reflection on the outside.

Insecurities ruled my appearance and behavior, lack of trust poised me for trouble, and fears led to long, sleepless nights. The truth was, I was broken. I partied for approval, sought self-worth in artificial relationships, and used addiction to cover up the horrible disaster churning inside. I craved attention for all the wrong reasons, sought affection to fill voids, and searched for affirmation of my worth from the world, the same world that told me I wasn't good enough. I was lost, miserable, and fatally wounded by sin. I was mistreated, devalued and mocked. I was helpless and hopeless.

His grace sheds light on the greatest darkness we carry.

I defined myself by my choices and wore them as a badge of shame.

When I was nineteen, God's grace provided a way out through salvation. It didn't change my past but choosing to follow Jesus shattered the lies Satan held over my head. The grip of the enemy on our lives can be tight, but the power of the Gospel is stronger. The gospel can break chains we didn't even know we had.

His grace sheds light on the greatest darkness we carry.

We set out for perfection only to find we fall short every time. Our hope is that God loves to use a mess for His glory. You see, only God can turn our worst moments into testimonies of grace.

God knows our need for perfection is false hope. No matter how hard we try, perfection is an outrageous lie. Striving for it only leads to brokenness and chaos. A mess looking for grace can only find redemption in the gospel. Like that old, worn piece of furniture we keep refinishing because to us it is priceless, God sees us as more than the mess we are. To Him we are worth refinishing into something beautiful.

It's Messy

Over the last few years, several catchphrases have been coined about being a mess; the ones which give us license to wear a messy bun and yoga pants in Target or pajamas to Walmart - can I get an amen? As women we eat up the glorification of a mess because well…most of us are one (whether we are willing to admit it or not). We love the fact that suddenly we can allow ourselves to call out the mess in our lives and wear it proudly. (Plus, I love anything that gives me a reason to live in my sweatpants.)

But, what about the other 'messes'? You know the ones I mean, those long-hidden or shoved-way-back-in-the-closet-of-our-hearts kind. They take many forms from imperfection and grief to overwhelming anxiety. Let's not fail to mention our extreme brokenness, as well as our addictions, failures as moms, issues in our marriages, and our desire to be heard in this noisy world.

When our weaknesses are laid out in front of us, it is no wonder we try to hide them because they are gross. We believe the lie that God wants nothing to do with the mess we have become. The longer the list of weaknesses, the less useful we see ourselves being for the Kingdom.

But, then there is grace.

The beauty comes when we hand over our weaknesses to our faithful Father and He turns them into usable strengths through His power. Areas of my life I never thought I would hand over to God have become things He has used the most. In our weakness is where He is strongest. I will never be perfect, and thankfully God doesn't require my perfection, because His power thrives in my weakness.

"But he said to me, "My grace is sufficient for you, for my power is made perfect in weakness." Therefore, I will boast all the more gladly of my weaknesses, so that the power of Christ may rest upon me" (2 Corinthians 12:9).

He changed and transformed me with power and purpose to display Him - to display His grace. Grace that is messy, yet utterly perfect, grace that leaves evidence of itself wherever it goes - not because of who I am, but because of who He is and the work He is doing within me. And, He will do the same for you.

Even though I still crave perfection, approval, and at times question if I am enough, God has changed my heart. He took my broken sinfulness and transformed it into something useful. You see, the holy part has nothing to do with you or me.

Like a good episode of Chopped where the chef is given a basket of items that don't make sense individually but somehow when combined result in a beautiful dish, when we bring our jumbled weaknesses to the table, God brings the holy, and the finished product is something amazing and useful.

God is capable of doing something in us we have no power to do ourselves.

The root of our mess starts with sin. We cannot overlook this fact - our sinfulness needs grace. We need Jesus because there is no other cure, there is no other way.

The answer to our sins, circumstances, and hurts is the power of Christ, and that is the gospel truth. The places we feel the weakest are where He shows up with all of His immeasurable power. We are complete in the grace of God; we still fall short and, at times, fail, but we find forgiveness and healing in Him alone. We can hold our heads high as His beloved daughters and proclaim the truth that the gospel changes everything.

There are some other women I know who are Holy-Mess, gospel-sharing truth tellers. They started broken, but God put each shattered part into His greater masterpiece. He transformed their stories into ones that will change us too.

The Bible is filled with women who experienced real life, doubts, questions, and disappointments, and we will see our own reflections in their lives. At least to their benefit they didn't have social media to compound their already fragile hearts.

Many women in Scripture teach us how the gospel changes everything. These kindred sisters were placed in God's narrative to accomplish specific purposes planned out for them individually. I want us to look past merely what we see on the surface; I want to jump straight into the thick of it with them. I want us to witness how the grace of God changed their lives and unveiled their identity in Him.

You, sitting on the other side of these pages, yes you, your life will be a living, breathing testimony of what being transformed by grace looks like. Your life is no mistake. When another woman looks at you, she will see the power of the gospel, even if she cannot explain what it is. God will use you and all those vulnerable, hazardous places in your life to tell the world about Him just like the women in the coming pages.

Does that surprise you? It should, but in the best kind of way. As I met with these women in the pages of Scripture, it painted a new picture of the words in Romans 8:28, "For we know that all things work together for good, for those who love God, and are called according to His purpose."

The car accident changed me; it shaped me. In something ugly and painful God revealed His purpose. God allowed it to teach me to stop hiding my broken, ugly messes and fight for truth. When we embrace truth, God's grace turns our lives into a message. It becomes about the Holy power of the gospel, rather than the disaster we are.

Every time I bring the mess, He is faithful to bring the holy.

Every time I seek forgiveness, He is faithful and just to forgive.

Every time I hurt, He is faithful to comfort.

Each woman in Scripture will show us the beautiful, awe-inspiring power of redemption and pure grace.

Journey with me and the women of the Bible as we take a look at what the gospel does with our mess. Each chapter will introduce a new dynamic woman from the sacred pages of Scripture. We will join her in the midst of her chaos, and witness how God's grace made her a woman radically changed by the gospel.

The Messes We Make

We are natural mess makers. Our mistakes, sinful hearts, brokenness, and need for perfection are what proves our need for Jesus.

CHAPTER ONE

The Mess of Our Mistakes

Eve (Genesis 1-3)

The heat was thick, my ankles were swollen, and I quickly began to realize taking a vacation while nine months pregnant was not the greatest idea I'd ever had. I spent days reassuring myself it was no big deal. Toes in the sand and ocean breezes sounded far better than lying on the couch unable to move because every muscle, ligament, and fiber of my body was screaming under the pressure of baby number three.

I will reluctantly confess I am a horrible pregnant woman. Would you believe me if I said my husband made me write that? It's ok. I'll own up to it.

Nevertheless, there we were a few hours into our vacation when it began to unravel. I had already waddled up the stairs of the beach house and found my spot on the couch, and there would be no future movement until I could regain proper oxygen levels. Well, that was until the phone rang. There is nothing like hearing your doctor on the other end, letting you know your levels (of some sort of fancy medical term I cannot remember) are high and preterm labor is an extreme possibility.

Really?

That's perfect.

Said no one, ever.

Preterm labor prescriptions, crying kids, a big pregnant woman, and an exhausted husband equaled a huge vacation mistake. I probably should have thought this through. But, the pinnacle of the error, however, was deciding we were brave enough to go shopping. Clearly, I momentarily lost all reason and thought, "It's 100 degrees outside, I can't move very quickly, and we have two whining kids. This will make for a winning night."

(This would be the part of the movie when the dramatic music begins to build.)

We pulled into the parking lot of the outlets and noticed a band of clouds coming awfully close. My husband looked at my belly and then into my eyes, "If we move fast maybe we will get in before it rains." The hormones in me wanted to say something else, but what left my mouth was something along the sarcastic lines of, "Yea, let's do that." No sooner had the car doors locked behind us when I felt the first drops followed immediately by an intense downpour. I looked up to find my husband and two children sprinting across the parking lot, leaving the massively pregnant and slow-moving wife and mother behind to save herself.

When I finally stepped inside the little shop they had taken refuge in, my hair was dripping, my clothes were drenched, and my three stared back at me barely touched by a drop of rain. My wonderful husband looked up at me as I came through the door, smiled slyly and asked, "Did you get wet?" Not a moment later my six-year-old chimed in, "Mom, did you see it's raining?"

Nope, I must have missed that.

It was an infamous vacation, a mistake we laugh about often at the dinner table. The mistake came in choosing something that had no chance of ending well; clearly, some choices aren't worth the trouble they bring.

I think most of us can pinpoint bad decisions we have made, anything from going on vacation at nine months pregnant to a choice that carried far more severe consequences than being stuck outside in the rain. Each day all of our actions and responses involve making a choice and, for better or worse, each one will have an impact. No one can claim to be mistake-free; we are flesh after all.

Being vulnerable means letting go of our pride and allowing God to be glorified.

If I gave you a piece of paper and asked you to write out every mistake, wrong choice, and moment of disobedience in your life, chances are you would respond like I did when I sat down to write this chapter - your insides would begin to cringe. There are not enough candy bars in the world to ease the thought of someone knowing every wrong turn I took in life. We don't want anyone to know the bad things about our past, or even our present, for that matter.

We pull down the shade over our vulnerability and sit in the dark alone for fear of what others would dare think of the mess we hide. Being vulnerable means letting go of our pride and allowing God to be glorified. Our scars aren't just for us to stare at. They have a purpose.

The vulnerable scars we cover up detail mistakes that most likely had enormous consequences. We have all made one choice in our lives that resulted in an outcome we still regret. Whether we like to say it out loud or not, our decisions have caused earthquakes in our homes, split relationships, broken people we love, and even destroyed reputations.

When we get to the root of our choices, let's be real, most of them stem from outright disobedience and even selfishness.

I have chosen my way more than a time or two and left a puddle of worthless excuses along the way. I believed what I wanted would fit right into God's plan, or at least He would eventually bend my way if I pushed hard enough. Like the voice on the other side of the navigation system, if you don't take the road it chooses, she may bug you for a little bit, but eventually, she will recalculate to a new direction.

God isn't a genie in a bottle we can shake and ask for wishes. He is far more powerful than what we have made up in our minds. He is the God of purpose and power; He is the One who set forth your direction before the beginning of time.

You can't get a better lesson in choices and consequences than Eve - she is the queen of consequences. Eve was made perfectly by God, but despite that fact she was not exempt from the devastation mistakes can leave in their wake. Eve was a Holy Mess, the first one to face heartaches, insecurities, and brokenness. The crushing blow of her story began to pave the way for the need of Christ and the redemptive power of the gospel.

If the first woman who ever walked this earth dealt with being a mess, then rest assured you are not alone where you are. There is no doubt in my mind as Eve laid her head down at night she wondered what she should have done differently, and what life would have been like if she had simply told the serpent, "No." I wonder if she wrapped her identity up in that one choice, if it became who she was - the woman who ate the forbidden fruit, gave it to her husband, Adam, and experienced the horror as sin became a part of our world.

"For as by the one man's disobedience the many were made sinners, so by the one man's obedience the many will be made righteous" (Romans 5:19).

One Choice

"In the beginning, God created the heavens and the earth" (Genesis 1:1).

He existed amid the unformed darkness, but He envisioned a world before Him, and by His power, God spoke into existence all things. What was nothing became something only at the magnificent sound of God's voice. He created the rugged dry land, glorious crashing waves, and rhythmic ocean. He formed colorful fish to swim in the seas and majestic birds to grace His piercingly blue sky.

God spoke, and trees formed as grass rose up from the dry, barren ground. Flowers of every hue and shape burst along riverbanks. God spoke the sun into its place and whispered the stars into the heavens. All creation was formed by His gracious hand and reverently whispered His name. But, that wasn't enough.

God cupped the dirt within His hands, shaping, molding, and forming man; He breathed life within the man's dry lungs and opened his eyes to life on Earth. This man was created to reflect the incredible image of God Himself.

God saw Adam's need for a helper, ally, and companion. So, from Adam's rib, God created her. He shaped her perfectly, breathed life into her body and presented her to the man.

Adam had not asked for her, but through grace, God saw the man's need for her. Eve, so carefully and gracefully constructed by God's hand, was the last thing created by the Father and placed into creation.

Nothing else was fashioned in nature the way she was. God crafted every ounce of her shape and beauty into the woman who would perfectly compliment her husband.

God placed her in a garden overflowing with lush plants and marvelously green, supple trees filled with an abundance of delicious fruits. Adam, who called her "bone of my bones and flesh of my flesh" (Genesis 2:23), treasured her and walked with her on that sacred ground.

The world was perfect and lacked nothing. There was no pain, no sadness, and no death. It was a world untainted by the cruelty of sin, and it is almost impossible for us to wrap our minds around the picture of what that perfect world looked like.

As Adam and his wife walked on fresh ground crafted by God's hands, I can only imagine their curiosity as they discovered exotic flowers and trees filled with incredible fruits. They stared at animals so uniquely designed that only a creative God could have formed them.

There was perfect peace. Picture them sitting together on the bank of a beautiful river in peace and stillness with no worries, no problems, and no stress. Their world was perfect, and unlike ours, they knew no anger, devastation, or sadness.

We know these truths about Eve and her husband from Scripture - their world was without sin; God created them in His image; they were made with purpose, value, and intention; and God, Himself, placed them in the garden (Genesis 1:27-2:8).

While she walked in the garden with God, Eve didn't struggle with comparison, defeat, or her body size. She knew Him in a way we will never be able to comprehend this side of Heaven. I imagine God spoke gently to her, taught her and loved her, and in return, she listened, learned, and loved Him back. There was no mess or imperfections to entangle Eve's heart and mind and separate her from her Holy God.

But, when the enemy came calling, he enticed Eve to question her contentment and worth. Satan left her believing she could be enough on her own and convinced her to question her Creator. The deceptive snake shifted her focus from God to the possibility of being perfect apart from Him. When she ate the forbidden fruit, Eve chose to believe who God made her to be wasn't enough. With her choice came shame, guilt, comparison, and all the other baggage that accompanies sin.

One bite unraveled her communion with God, and with it her perfect peace.

One bite unraveled her communion with God, and with it her perfect peace.

When Eve's focus changed from the grace of God to her efforts, she set herself up for defeat.

The paradise they knew became radically altered by sin; there wasn't an ounce of creation that was not touched or changed by the immediate darkness. As soon as the fruit was eaten, shame fell, and their innocence was utterly ripped away. Suddenly, what was perfect was now flawed; what was whole abruptly became incomplete.

This explosive truth should jolt us - a simple deception led to the world's corruption! The enemy simply made Eve believe she could have the knowledge of good and evil and, in essence, be like God. Satan even went a step further to entice her by twisting and manipulating God's Word. We don't have to look far to see him desperately trying to seduce us with the same lies.

The enemy wants to keep you wrapped up in your sinful choices and mistakes. He wants to deceive you into believing you are ok there in your pit of destruction.

Don't believe for a moment you are an exception to a lying enemy. He is content with us stuck in a pit of misery, struggling and striving for perfection. The enemy wants nothing more than for us to believe his lies rather than God's truth. He sneaks his way into our weakness and mess and causes us to think there is no way God can fix us, much less use us. Satan wants you to believe you are better off on your own.

Eve may have felt the sting of God's justice, but she also experienced the majesty of His grace.

Eve's lack of obedience and choosing her own way left broken relationships, broken lives, and a broken world. One choice of disobedience shifted everything from perfection to destruction. Eve certainly never imagined what the result would be when she and Adam chose to disobey God's command. That is the thing about sin, we never fully understand the consequences until it is too late. Our willingness to rebel against what He has asked us to do can even result in ramifications which can extend for generations.

You and I are the same as Eve in that our choice to obey or disobey what God has commanded of us looks no different. Of course, our choices will not cause the fall of man, but that is no license for us to continue down a path of disobedience. Nothing justifies our turning away from God.

Eve's story is a warning to us to live an obedient life, but it also displays incredible hope for when we fail. Eve may have felt the sting of God's justice, but she also experienced the majesty of His grace.

In the Mirror

For many years of my life, I believed I was no better than my worst mistake. I felt defined by every choice I made. I was sure that when someone looked at me, they saw every misstep and wrong turn I had taken in my life. I believed it was just who I was, a walking billboard of my sin. I thought I would never be known as anything different. Even after I gave my life to Christ, I felt the emotions and weight of the mess I had made in my past. I questioned God, "How can you love me? Change me? Use a mess like me?"

The woman I see every morning reminds me of Eve. She desperately tries to be enough on her own and ends up exhausted from a week of trying to live up to worldly expectations. She is bogged down with not getting it all done - from the piles of laundry sitting on the floor to the endless demands of the people around her. She hides her lonely places, hurts, and insecurities behind carefully constructed walls. She conceals the brokenness in her marriage, her relationship failures, and her difficulties at work or with her children. She fears her mess is too much for anyone else to handle and compares herself at every turn. Do you see her too?

The deception of perfection causes the infection of comparison.

The deception of perfection causes the infection of comparison.

When our worn-out bodies and overwhelmed souls get a few moments of peace, we grab our phones and begin to scroll. We see perfectly posed pictures, Pinterest-worthy meals, and stylish outfits we only wish we could wear. We see poised moms who look like they probably rolled out of bed flawless and we wonder if God just made them perfect.

We absorb endless words detailing the illusion of perfect lives and perfect children. If you are like me, you're sitting there in your yoga pants wondering if you're doing it all wrong. Did God make her perfect and forget about me?

The enemy is whispering, and we are buying into his trickery.

We want the world to think we are enough and we have it all figured out. We scramble quickly to put together something resembling profound and perfect, snap a picture and post it out there in the social media universe. We wait. We hope deep down for an abundance of likes and comments filled with approval and validation of our worth as a woman, wife, and mother.

What are we doing?! We are making the same mistake of believing the enemy's lies just like Eve. We have to stop looking for our worth in all the wrong places. It wasn't found in the fruit, and it definitely won't be found on our screens.

Eve was unprepared for the cunning liar that slithered his way into her life. Remember there was no sin or darkness in her world, but there is in ours. Don't let your mistakes come from a lack of preparation against the very enemy Eve's story teaches us to be aware of. Don't be naive enough to believe he won't slither into your life as well.

The serpent was cunning in his deception. With one question he made Eve doubt what God said and question His motives. He does the same to us - Satan makes us question the motives and direction of God in our lives. We ask ourselves, "Why has God placed me in this unknown season? Why is He putting all of this on me? Did He really say not to do this? Am I really happy in my marriage? Don't I deserve more?"

"The desire when it has conceived gives birth to sin, and sin when it is fully grown brings forth death" (James 1:15).

Eve took matters into her own hands when the enemy tricked her into believing she needed more. And it left her, and us, in a sinful mess. Often our desire to be enough is what crushes us. Eve may have been the first woman to walk this earth, but no woman is an exception to the enemy's deception.

She believed the fruit was the answer to the longing she felt in her heart. Rather than seeing the constant love and grace of God, she chose to see what she could accomplish on her own. She looked to something misleading rather than the truth. Sound like anyone else you may know? To me it sounds a lot like the girl I see in the mirror.

God's grace repaints the narrative of our messes into a beautiful image of His love.

God's grace repaints the narrative of our messes into a beautiful image of His love. Grace took Eve from the despair of punishment to the hope of life. Her story didn't end with sin, even though throughout Eve's very long life she faced struggle after struggle. She dealt with shame and what we can assume was great regret for the choices she had made. There was nothing simple about her life as the mother of humankind.

Due to sin, Eve undoubtedly was the first to experience many of the disappointments you and I face today. Motherhood came with its fair share of grief and struggle for her, but stick with me; it's about to get good.

Once removed from the garden, she and Adam faced a new life; a hard life of toil, trouble, and turmoil.

God gave this couple the command to multiply and start the first family. Maybe you know the story, but if you aren't familiar, here are the basics. They had two sons – Cain and Abel. Each one brought their offerings to God. Cain brought the fruit of his hands that he labored for while Abel brought the firstborn of his flock. God rejected the offering of Cain, and in Cain's anger, he killed his brother.

This wasn't to say the offering of a herdsman was greater than that of a farmer. No, we have to look deeper. A telling truth about God is found in 1 Samuel 16:7, "But the LORD said to Samuel, "Do not look on his appearance or on the height of his stature, because I have rejected him." For the LORD sees not as man sees; man looks on the outward appearance, but the LORD looks on the heart."

It wasn't the offering that was a problem, it was the posture of the giver's heart. Cain's heart was evil, while Abel brought his offering with a humble heart. "We should not be like Cain, who was of the evil one and murdered his brother. And why did he murder him? Because his own deeds were evil and his brother's righteous" (1 John 3:12).

Evidence of the fall in the garden came in the murder of a brother.

Despite the awful loss of her son, we begin to see God unfold redemption in Eve's story through another son.

"And Adam knew his wife again, and she bore a son and called his name Seth, for she said, 'God has appointed for me another offspring instead of Abel, for Cain killed him.' To Seth also a son was born, and he called his name Enosh. At that time people began to call upon the name of the Lord" (Genesis 4:25- 26).

Seth, whose name means *established*, was used by God to begin the holy line that would lead to the birth of Redemption, Jesus Christ.

God had no intention of leaving His beloved children in their shame. He was, and is, ready and willing to extend grace, not just for her mess alone, but for all humanity. Eve witnessed His grace through her son Seth. Her lineage and legacy would ultimately crush the same serpent who deceived her by bringing forth the Promised One. We look at her and see God's incredible hand shaping her story.

One greater would come from Eve to fulfill the words of God from the garden. "I will put enmity between you and the woman, and between your offspring and her offspring; he shall bruise your head, and you shall bruise his heel" (Genesis 3:15). The fall in the garden was not the end of the story. Jesus was coming to right every wrong.

There is no mistake that Eve is the first woman we meet in Holy Mess because she was a mess like you and me. Her life was the first to feel the sting of the enemy's lies and suffer the consequences. She teaches us that despite our shortcomings and mess ups, God's grace is more than enough.

The enemy wants to deceive you just as he did Eve. He wants you to believe you have to be enough on your own. We have to stand firm in God's truth that God sent His Son, Jesus, to be enough for us all.

Enough for every failure, mistake, and wrong choice.

Enough for every insecurity, rejection, and broken heart.

Enough for every grief, sickness, and weakness.

Enough to be our hope and salvation alone.

What little we know about Eve's life after they left the garden can only be left to speculation. But, what we do know is more important than what we don't know. Eve's story didn't stay wrapped up in her mistake because God transformed her wreckage into a story that transcends all of time. It doesn't change the mistake that was made, but it does prove God can and will right every wrong.

A vacation that turned out badly pales in comparison to what we will face and what Eve faced. It is, however, an earthly reminder that the gospel is enough even when we are at our lowest.

The redemptive grace of Christ is what transforms a life. We cannot save, redeem, or change ourselves, only God can do that. His grace changes and transforms the story of our lives and takes us from brokenness to complete wholeness, from a messed up past to a useable future. Grace is more than just a one-time gift, it is a daily outpouring from God for every situation and circumstance - for every person, everywhere.

Eve's messy mistake resulted in God's punishment, but she also experienced the power of His perfect grace. And, you can too.

CHAPTER TWO
The Mess of Brokenness

The Bleeding Woman and the Samaritan Woman
(Matthew 9:20-22; John 4:6-42)

One of my most cherished memories with my dad was our time on the beach together. There will always be something about the fresh bite of ocean air against my face and the white tops of the rolling waves that reminds me of him, our walks, and laughter. Many long talks about life happened on those sandy mounds. Even now, I close my eyes when I stand at the ocean and can almost hear him and feel him close.

As an adult, taking my children to the ocean brings me such joy, creating the same memories with them that I shared with my father. Every time my feet dig into the warm, grainy sand and the breeze sweeps across my face, it takes me to another place. It takes me to a season of my life when my dad taught me how to collect shells, all different kinds, each with its own beautiful shape and color. We would fill bags to the top with every shell we could find. Each one was a treasure, not because of its appearance but because I found it while I was with my father.

I watch my children scurry down the beach with bags and buckets in hand, looking, searching for bits of treasure waiting there.

The joy of finding large, beautiful shells waiting to be picked up is as thrilling to them as it was for me when I was a child.

When the kids were little there was no shell off limits - if it fit in the bucket it was a treasure worth picking up. I began to notice they would race to the mountains of broken shells, lift them up and declare how beautiful each one was. To my husband and I, the shells were nothing more than broken rubble. There wasn't much that was beautiful about what they held in their hands.

But, each of those shells didn't start broken; at one point they were perfectly whole and beautiful. However, as the waves tossed and crashed from raging storms and turbulent seas, they began to crack, chip, and shatter leaving only fragments behind of what they once were.

Sound familiar? Does the brokenness of the shells resemble pieces of your own life? It sure sounds like mine.

Life sometimes tosses us around like a hurricane with towering waves crashing down on us without warning.

Those storms leave us a broken fragment of the whole beauty we used to be.

Sometimes the waves are ones we cause ourselves, but the results are the same, one more crack, one more break that leaves us not recognizing the woman we used to be. Just like the shells on the beach, we become a broken mess.

Brokenness in our own hands only produces ashes.

Sadly, we view storm-ravaged people the way we see cast-off shells; we turn away from their brokenness and reject what they've become. But, the truth is each one of us is broken, incomplete, and filled with cracks and chips. We try our best to hide the hurts and mess and won't allow anyone to see our pain. The ugliness isolates us from our friends and leaves us feeling unworthy and unlovable.

We cannot hide our brokenness, no matter how hard we try.

We are broken people underneath it all, and broken people need the gospel. Think about it, if we were perfectly whole we wouldn't need a Savior.

Like the beach filled with broken shells, Scripture is full of broken women. In the New Testament we see the accounts of two women with very different stories but similar broken hearts. Sin sent one woman to the town well at the hottest time of day to avoid anyone who might call her out for her transgressions. The other woman was so desperate for freedom from her condition that she went looking secretly for healing from Jesus in the middle of a crowd.

The Well

The sun blazed high in the sky with heat so intense it penetrated her skin and formed beads of sweat on her brow. The weight of the warm clay water jar on her head slowed her steps but didn't deter her from her purpose because she knew the well would be clear of the other women. No doubt they were inside seeking shelter from the heat of the day. As she walked, she sighed with the weight of being alone. This is where her sin had brought her.

Living in the desert meant women would wait for early morning or dusk when the weather was cooler to draw from the well. This Samaritan woman felt she had no choice but to go to the well during the midday heat when no one was around. Her heart probably couldn't bear the stares and whispers of her neighbors. A lonely life was better than a mocked life.

She likely checked over her shoulder to make sure no one was coming. Avoiding the judging stares and hateful whispers became her mission. Her neighbors only saw a broken, sinful wretch. What they didn't see was her painful despair and broken heart.

With every step, the words that had been said about her began to fill her mind as the enemy whispered to her, "Your life is a devastating wreck. You will always be a mess." Words hurled at her over the years of her indiscretions weighed on her heart, and she sadly claimed them as her identity. She felt unworthy, unlovable, and dirty. She began to believe this was her lot in life. Shame had become her name.

It was my name too.

Make no mistake, when the Son of God chose His spot at the well, He knew what He was doing. When Jesus reached out to the ones who were deemed unfit in Jewish eyes, He showed the masterfully painted picture of the gospel. God, Himself, unfolded the truth that Jesus came for all humanity.

The fact that this woman had a mountain of sin to her name didn't stop Him from sharing hope with her. We cannot skip these details - we cannot gloss over the ugly parts of her story because they reveal just how great His grace is.

By cultural standards this woman had no place even speaking to Jesus. He was a Jewish man while she was a sinful Samaritan woman. Their conversation broke all the rules of both cultures. God, however, is not limited by cultural or religious practices - nothing stops Him from reaching His children.

Reasonably, she questioned Him, "How is it that you, a Jew, ask for a drink from me, a Samaritan woman?" (John 4:9). Oh, friend, His response started a conversation that changed the way she spent the rest of her life. God knew her, this sinful woman, who came to draw from the well. Jesus chose not to address the cultural issue because petty differences obstruct the truth of the gospel. He came straight to the point, "If you knew the gift of God, and who says to you 'Give me a drink,' you would have asked Him, and He would have given you living water" (John 4:10). Here was a broken woman more worried about what made the two of them so different rather than 'seeing' the truth sitting in front of her. Jesus cast the racial remark aside as trivial and focused instead on the importance found in the Living Water He offered her.

Jesus revealed her sin and provided Himself as the Remedy.

She felt the pull of desire for the water that gave Life and would keep her from ever thirsting again. Before any Life-giving water could be provided, He had to lay her mess bare. No sins can remain hidden to the eyes of God, to the Living Water who came to save. He didn't withhold the truth from this hurting woman. Jesus revealed her sin and provided Himself as the Remedy.

In the heat of the day at the town well, Jesus was offering the sacrifice of His life for hers. He knew her heart with all its sin and shame, just as He knows ours. His piercing words cut deep to the root of her brokenness, "Go, call your husband to come here" (John 4:16). He was not going to let her walk away until He addressed her mess.

Her response revealed a truth Christ knew already, she had no husband. What she did have was a reputation for being with many men - five to be exact. God's intention for sex is clear, it is to remain within the confines of marriage alone (Exodus 20:14, 1 Thessalonians 4:3-5, Hebrews 13:4, Genesis 2:24-25). Her actions had broken the law, but more than that, it had broken the heart of God. Unlike the whispers of those around her, when Christ pointed out her sinful stains, He offered her cleansing.

Healing Faith

Not every mess is one we create ourselves; some circumstances are out of our control. Just because we didn't cause it, doesn't mean we don't need to be redeemed by grace from it. In the case of the bleeding woman in Mark 5, her brokenness wasn't caused by her own hands but was used for a great purpose.

Can you imagine the talk in the streets of Jesus' miracles? There is no doubt word went out before Him. They spoke of His teachings on the mountainsides and in the synagogues, and many who witnessed these things believed Jesus was the true Messiah. I wonder if she heard the whispers and knew in her heart that this was her chance for healing - Jesus, the Messiah, could save her from the disease that had taken over her body.

Twelve years she had suffered at the hands of this excruciating and humiliating ailment, losing everything because of it. Scripture, after all, was clear, a woman with a flow of blood was unclean and was not to be touched (Leviticus 15:19-30).

Which meant twelve years without contact.

Without connection.

Every item in her home - her furniture, her clothing, and her body - were all unclean by the standards of the religious.

Her bleeding never ceased and as a result her body was worn and exhausted. She would see a new doctors and hold out hope that they could help her, but the answer was the same each time. Nothing barring a miracle would offer an escape from this torture she found herself in.

For so long she had been called unworthy, unlovable, and untouchable. Surely, thinking of approaching Christ raised many emotions. Would this Messiah, a Jew, look at her the same as all the rest – disgusting and unclean? She believed so strongly that she had to try no matter what happened to her afterward. All she knew in her heart was that touching Him, even just brushing a small piece of His clothing, would radically change and heal her from her brokenness.

In desperation she stretched out her tired, shaking hands as the crowd pressed against Him - just one touch. Fingers stretched as far as she could take them, and then finally, she touched the edge of the Messiah's long robe.

What faith she had in His power to heal, that by simply touching His robe she would be made whole!

"And he looked around to see who had done it. But the woman, knowing what had happened to her, came in fear and trembling and fell down before him and told him the whole truth" (Mark 5:32).

Jesus knew immediately someone had touched him. The woman who was shamed and cast out for her condition stood face to face with the One who came to restore and heal. Crumbling at His feet in fear that He, too, would cast her out as unclean, she told Him the truth.

He redeemed her mess and restored her as righteous.

His response to this broken woman was that her faith had healed her. Jesus had freed her from her suffering.

He redeemed her mess and restored

her as righteous.

Each of the miracles Christ performed gives us a small glimpse of the transformation He completes in us. This woman, who by the world's standards was an unworthy cast-off, allows us to see that God looks past our condition to see deep within our hearts. He sees our faith and takes us from broken to complete, cast out to welcomed in.

He already knows your pain before you even step into His presence.

"But God, being rich in mercy, because of the great love with which he loved us, even when we were dead in our trespasses, made us alive together with Christ by grace you have been saved" (Ephesians 2:4).

Have you ever reached that place of desperate brokenness?

A place where you take cautious steps to avoid further landmines in your life? Then suddenly, in what seems like a strange and unlikely place, you encounter Jesus. He takes your hand and enables you to step out of your broken despair into wholeness.

Both women had a desperate thirst for Living Water that could only be satisfied by Jesus. One knew where to find it, but the other didn't recognize it until it was offered. Jesus didn't leave them holding on to their brokenness; the water jar was left at the well and the sickness was left at Jesus' feet.

He already knows your pain before you even step into His presence.

Psalm 147:3 says, "He hears the broken-hearted and binds up their wounds."

This promise is fulfilled in the person of Jesus Christ who came to bind up the broken hearted, the shattered in spirit, and the crushed from sin.

Our fractured hearts can only be mended by His healing hand.

When we take our eyes off the mangled places in our lives and turn them to His incredible grace, we will stop seeing the cracks and chips we received in the storms. We will start seeing the immensely beautiful purpose and promise God has set before us. The woman at the well hid her broken places from the world, while the bleeding woman could barely bring herself through the crowd. Each woman was different, but the result was the same. They needed grace to be healed and restored, and to remind them they are a treasure to God. We don't hear anything else about these women after their encounters with Jesus, but we can venture a good guess they were never the same.

Brokenness Redeemed

Don't believe for a second our mighty Father cannot use your brokenness, or believe the lie from the enemy that you are too broken to be used of God.

There was another moment I spent on the beach, but this time with my Heavenly Father. God taught me something I will never forget one spring afternoon after the deepest heartache of our second miscarriage.

I felt discarded like those damaged shells, tossed aside and unseen. That was until my daughter raced toward me with a broken shell in hand, "Mommy, mommy, look how beautiful. I just love the broken ones." At that moment, God whispered in the breeze off of the ocean water and deep into my heart, "Me, too."

Despite the pain I felt, I wasn't discarded or tossed aside. I was seen in my brokenness and I was loved, valued, and beautiful in the eyes of my Father.

Even though we come tossed ashore cracked, shattered, and discarded, God collects us with excitement and tenderly places us in His 'bucket'.

He sees potential when the world sees unfixable.

He sees beauty when the world sees broken.

He sees useful when the world sees useless.

God loves broken people full of weaknesses and imperfections. In His economy He values us as priceless treasures worth dying for.

Like my children on the beach who reach for the broken shells, God reaches for us in our mess. He sees what we used to be and, in His incredible grace, He knows just what we can be through His power.

You don't have to remain a broken mess, allow God's grace to transform you and call you holy.

CHAPTER THREE

The Mess of Sin

The Sinful Woman (Luke 7:36-50)

When I was a teenager, I vividly remember telling a classmate God wasn't real. The thought of that moment now makes me cringe. I laughed at and mocked those who called the wrong I did, sin. It had no effect and carried no weight - at least not at that moment.

The older I became, the heavier the burden I carried. The weight of the shame and guilt crushed me so that I was overtaken. What I once spent so much time denying was beginning to suffocate the desperate places of my heart that screamed out for healing. God brought me to a place where I was so undone by my sin, and He opened my eyes to see that He alone could free me from it.

There was a time in my life when freedom was illusive. My cycle of habits began to destroy me, and my purpose in life became a race to fill the gaping holes in my heart. What I failed to see was those missing pieces were God-shaped, and everything I tried to fill the gaps with only left wounds bigger than before.

I wish I could paint a pretty picture of my life before Christ, but I can't. There is no way to turn something ugly into something beautiful on my own.

What makes us a mess is the sin that wraps around our insides over time - choosing alcohol over healing, drugs over a reckoning, and immorality over the love of God.

This kind of mess separates us from Christ.

Our holy, righteous Heavenly Father comes to rescue and redeem us from sin. This divine intervention is a reckoning for the life we used to live and a transformation of our future.

Sin is messy, but more than that, it wants you bound and destroyed. Crippling bondage steered my teenage years, and I spent my days seeking anything that would make me feel loved. My life soon spiraled out of control. My sin became my identity while my wrong choices defined who I was. My life wasn't what I hoped it would be, but that's the thing about sin, it's never what we expect. It infects like a rapidly spreading disease, a virus out of control with only one cure.

I was filled with shame, and it caused me to believe I would always be unlovable and beyond help. Satan had me trapped in my darkest fear because he knows the quickest way to ensure a woman's heart is to make her feel beyond the reach of love.

But, here is the truth - sin didn't have the final say in my life, and it doesn't have to for you either.

God sought to change my story. I knew my life was filled with darkness and deeply broken, but it wasn't until a woman I knew at the time shared the words, "God saved me," that a light suddenly turned on. Illumination to the darkest places of my heart began to take place.

God used her story to speak straight to my lost heart. He saved me in spite of me, not for me, but for His holy purpose, to the praise of His glory.

"In him we have obtained an inheritance, having been predestined according to the purpose of him who works all things according to the counsel of his will, so that we who were the first to hope in Christ might be to the praise of his glory" (Ephesians 1:11-12).

I am saved and forgiven, but I battle sin every single day, and whether we want to admit it out loud or not, we all do. Sin is the most significant mess of all. I have and will continue to wrestle with sin and will daily need grace and forgiveness. As long as I am breathing and being sanctified by God, sin will be a part of the equation.

No one can accuse me of being perfect. I am wholly and utterly imperfect. So imperfect in fact that I am writing a book to help women come to terms with this fact in their lives.

He saved me in spite of me, not for me, but for His holy purpose, to the praise of His glory.

No one in the history of the world apart from Jesus was perfect. Let's rest in that.

Immeasurable Sin

She was wounded, not on the outside where anyone could see, but deep in her heart. Each gash was of her own making, revealing the transgressions that named her. The looks of disgust from her neighbors as she walked the dusty roads surely kept her trapped in the chains of shame. It would have forced her to believe that she would never be more than the sin she carried. I am certain there was a deep longing in her eyes, an ache to be loved from a woman deemed unlovable, if anyone dared to look long enough.

I am sure they stared at her as she walked through the streets. Men likely dared not look her way and be associated with her profession. No one knew or cared who she was apart from her sin. She had given up hope in people and religion; neither one had rescued her from her circumstance, but rather, both marked her as unwanted.

This sinful woman heard the whispers in the streets about this man Jesus. The city was filled with talk about the widow's son being raised from the dead. Surely this man they called a prophet wasn't like the other religious men because He displayed compassion for the hurting and addressed their hurts in ways never seen before. I wonder if she feared He would shun her just like all the others.

Jesus was magnetizing, drawing her to Him. She needed to see Him for herself. The light in Him revealed the darkness in her - a darkness that God was stirring in her to lay down. She may have stood in her house pouring over her possessions wondering what she could offer the One who forgives sins and restores the broken. The alabaster jar contained expensive perfume she could have possibly used to lure men into sin. This perfume her profession relied on to make a profit. This jar defined her life and represented her shame. Yes! This was what she would take and offer Jesus. This jar would be the evidence that she desired freedom more than staying bound in sin.

I can see her standing behind the pillar at the edge of the doorway gripping the jar in her hands trembling from the fear welling up in her. The repentant tears stung her eyes. When she saw Jesus reclining at the table, she moved quietly and slowly so as not to draw attention to herself. Every step she took saw her tears hit the ground, and she knew in her heart this Man held forgiveness in His hands. Standing behind

Him she fell to the ground with tears pouring from her eyes, heavy with the weight of guilt and sorrow.

Without hesitation, she broke the top of the alabaster jar and began to pour the precious oil on the feet of Jesus. Using her long, dark hair she gently wiped His feet and reverently kissed them again and again. The table grew silent as the guests watched this intimate scene. Jesus spoke not a word to her but willingly accepted her adoration.

I have visualized this scene in my mind many times when I read it in the pages of my Bible, haven't you? At times I wonder if this is a sweet taste of Heaven and the love I will be able to shower on Jesus' feet for the gift of salvation.

"For the word of the cross is foolishness to those who are perishing, but it is the power of God to us who are being saved" (1 Corinthians 1:18, CSB).

It was no wonder the keeper of the house was appalled by the actions of this woman touching Jesus. But, she never ceased her devotion despite their hurtful words. Her faith in Jesus was more important than the opinions of the Pharisees, and they WOULD NOT distract her heart from the only One who offered her forgiveness. Her need for repentance was more significant than their words.

Jesus suddenly spoke, and the room grew silent. He didn't look to the woman but to Simon, the host of the party, and began to tell the story of two debtors, one loaned a large amount of money and the other a smaller sum, yet both were forgiven of their debts by the lender.

Then Jesus asked Simon, "Which of them will love him more?" And his accurate response was, "I suppose the one who he forgave more" (Luke 7:43).

This woman of sin, whose transgressions were known to all within the city gates, and this man of high religious standing whose sin

This woman who wasn't even called by her name, found salvation in Christ alone, by grace alone

was hidden in his pride, were both equally sinners. Jesus addressed their need for forgiveness individually. Only one of them accepted the offer, and she left free. This woman who wasn't even called by name, found salvation in Christ alone, by grace alone.

Fully Loved

Right above my desk, I have a sign that I hand-lettered of Luke 7:47, "Her sins which were many are forgiven." Of all the women in this book, God has used her story to open my eyes to the truth of the gospel. We learn from her that forgiveness is not out of reach, no matter your sin or standing in this world. God looks at His daughters through the blood of Christ.

It is easy to steer clear of our wretched stories and hide who we used to be for fear of what others will think of us, or what they will say. There is nothing about my own story that isn't messy too. But friend, we should be fueled by vulnerability. When we raise our hand and admit our mess and that God alone has removed our shame, there is freedom not just for us, but also for someone else.

I don't mean vulnerability that verbally vomits all things on all people. I mean the willingness to raise a hand and not claim perfect, but messy.

For the sinful woman, her vulnerability meant walking into the room where Jesus was and facing the "religious" people who scorned and pointed their fingers at her. To them, this woman was nothing more than her sin.

Her exposed, repentant heart was more potent than the fear of facing her accusers. Jesus allowed this woman to touch His feet despite guests around the table who were confused by the action, and a host disgusted by her appalling behavior. Each one, blind to their own sins, failed to witness the beauty of forgiveness happening right in front of them.

Deep in her heart, however, the sinful woman was drawn to this man Jesus. She wept over Him, anointed His feet with precious oil, and used her hair, the beauty of her head, to wipe the feet of the Gospel - all because He loved and forgave her.

She was heavily bound by the sin she carried and the weight of her choices. The sin that sought to keep her in bondage was released to freedom in Jesus, the One who came to save sinners. The forgiveness of her sins wasn't a result of her actions. It was her faith that propelled her response. This woman who wept at Jesus' feet was the picture of the mess of sin and how we can't be changed apart from Christ.

The sinful woman displays the ultimate power of forgiveness that rests in God's hands alone.

There was no need for her to 'clean herself up' before coming to Christ. She landed at his feet worshipping the One who restored her soul. She knew the Source of forgiveness and grace, and her love for Him was reflected in her actions.

Without hesitation, she met her Redeemer's eyes and heard His words of forgiveness and peace, "Her sins, which are many, have been forgiven" (Luke 7:47). This sinful woman was no longer to be defined by her sin but by the glory of God she now manifested. The chains that once held her had been broken.

Jesus' offering of forgiveness was not flippant. Author and Pastor Warren Wiersbe reminds us, "His words weren't cheap words; they cost Him dearly on the cross."[1] We are unable to pay the debt of sin ourselves, but Jesus, our stand-in, offered Himself up for us. He extends the hand of forgiveness out to us; we act in faith to accept it. We are not saved by actions, (just as the woman wasn't redeemed for the act of anointing His feet), but by faith.

Ephesians 2:8-9, "For by grace are you saved through faith; not of yourselves, it is the gift of God: Not of works, so no one can boast."

Once washed in forgiveness, we can then step forward in peace.

Theologian Herbert Lockyer says this, "He accepted the woman's sobs and perfume as the pledge of a past forgiveness and the promise of a life to be lived for His glory."[2] The final words Jesus spoke to the woman were, "Your faith has saved you, go in peace" (Luke 7:50). Her faith saved her from sin, and the command of Jesus is to go in peace which is translated as "go into peace," a prompt to go into the new way she would live, in the peace of Christ.

His love for you is far beyond the understanding of our minds; it is the length and width of a wooden cross and the weight of the crown of thorns upon His head.

Philippians 4:7, "And the peace of God [that peace that reassures the heart, that peace] which transcends all understanding, [that peace which] stands guard over your hearts and your minds in Christ Jesus [is yours]" (AMP).

His hand of forgiveness is open to you and the cleansing for your mess is freely given. When we are ravaged by the despair of sin, we need a remedy and it is found in Christ alone. His love for you is far beyond the understanding of our minds; it is the length and width of a wooden cross and the weight of the crown of thorns upon His head.

The sinful woman knew there was nothing better than Jesus. I, too, learned that truth the day I surrendered my all to Him. I may not have been able to pour my oil and tears upon His feet physically, but I offered my life into His hands. I handed over the sin that sought to destroy me and went out in peace. And, so can you.

CHAPTER FOUR
The Mess of Perfection

Mary & Martha (Luke 10:38-42)

It is in the dairy aisle of Target, right near the coffee creamer, you see her - the woman who has it all together. She is truly astounding in all her beauty, with her well-behaved children, and a joyful smile. You suddenly feel gross and defeated. You quickly turn down a different aisle to avoid her seeing your Einstein hair, your kicking and screaming children, and the lack of joy that has settled into the fine lines on your face.

How is it that she has it together and you don't?

What are you doing wrong in your life that you look like a mess and she looks like perfection?

It's not just Sundays... It's Mondays and every other day that ends in "y." Most of us wake up with high expectations and a long list fluttering through our minds of what we need to accomplish, people to make happy, and appearances to keep up with. We spend the morning searching for the right outfit and making sure our hair doesn't show the evidence that it hasn't been washed all week (hence the creation of dry shampoo).

We have done all the planning in our pretty (and unbelievably expensive) planners, penned out meals for the week, packed lunches, and scheduled endless appointments. "Take that, Monday!" we say, "You are no match for my plan for perfection." But by 9:00 a.m. when the coffee is cold, you're running late, and your shoes are two different colors - you suddenly realize, Monday has won, and your hope of perfection has been tossed right out the window.

Fake perfection leaves us comparing our disaster to her smoke and mirrors.

The truth is, we are desperate to get it all right and have it all together, no matter the cost. We keep the messes tucked away from view while we polish and shine what's on the outside to keep up the illusion. Fake perfection leaves us comparing our disaster to her smoke and mirrors.

Mess-Maker

I cannot hide it; I am a notorious mess maker. My desk looks like a constant state of disarray, and if I am honest, the rest of my house looks the same way. There is no denying when spring cleaning rolls around (or when I am avoiding the book editing process) that my house will become a hub of purging, rearranging, and donating until my family is ready to donate me instead.

On average days, however, I want the house in order, but it never fails when I begin to deep clean, my children will ask, "Mom, who is coming over?" I know I am not the only one who hits the red alert button when someone even hints at coming to my house. Just think of the sheer level of panic you would feel if you knew Jesus was coming to hang out at your home for the afternoon. With my three children, there could be any number of disgusting things on the couch cushions where Jesus would sit. But, He would first have to make it past the tiny Legos on the floor and the laundry in the hallway stacked higher than my ceiling.

No sooner than Jesus set foot in my house, would the closet that hides all my junk burst open and display a greater disaster than I could even begin to explain. To make matters worse, if Jesus didn't like goldfish, gummy snacks, or peanut butter and jelly sandwiches, I am afraid I would have nothing else to offer Him to eat.

Knowing Jesus as I do, He would walk past the closet of terror, step over the Legos, brush the crumbs from the couch, take my hand and say, "Sit with me." You see, this perfection we crave isn't what God desires from us. All of the things we believe would keep Christ from being with us are really human-made distractions.

Striving for perfect leaves us drowning in failure.

Our starvation for perfection, if given enough time to take root, will cause a catastrophe in our lives. I am confident in this fact - striving for perfect leaves us drowning in failure.

We have let the enemy set us up to believe we need to clean ourselves up before we can be good enough for God. We cannot be good enough! Nothing we do will make us good enough - that is why we need Jesus.

"Not that we are sufficient in ourselves to claim anything as coming from us, but our sufficiency is from God" (2 Corinthians 3:5).

Jesus gives grace for our mess, hope for our distress, and mercy for our weakness.

If perfection was required there would be no need for the cross. No Instagram filter can change the truth - Jesus is the only One who changes everything when He steps into our lives.

Two Sisters

Jesus and His disciples traveled the countryside rarely staying in one place for very long. There were too many things that needed to be done, and Jesus knew His time was short. There were people to reach and teach, and people who needed healing and hope. By the time He reached the village of Bethany, Jesus had healed the sick and blind, and His teachings had become famous.

Mary and Martha would have known of Jesus. Talk of all He had done hit the sand of Bethany before His feet ever stepped through the gates. Who wouldn't jump at the chance for Jesus to enter their home? He was the Messiah whom they had waited so long for - He was their Rescuer.

I wonder if Martha was known for her hostess abilities? This would have been her chance to shine before the Messiah, giving Him nothing less than her best. If I imagine this story, I can see Martha scurrying to make things perfect - only the best dishes, the finest ingredients from the market and her best recipes would do. One thing was clear, she loved Him and was grateful for the chance to serve Him.

I can see her spending the better part of the day straightening and organizing her house. It needed to look perfect for Christ. The mats must be dusted, the table cleaned, and bowls of warm water placed near the door to wash their hands and feet. She would look around the room and point out the finest mat upon the floor and declare that this would be Jesus'. She would enter the room with her trays of abundant food, and Jesus would be pleased with her hard work.

She could hear it within her thoughts, "Well done Martha, how hard you have worked!" She would boast to herself, "Yes, Jesus will be so thankful for my hard work, He will see how hard I have tried to make it perfect for Him. He will know how much I love Him."

Mary would have stood in the doorway watching her sister. She did not understand the rush and busyness her sister seemed so concerned with. Mary couldn't believe the Savior would rest in her home where she would hear His voice and see His face for herself! This moment was more than she could have possibly asked for. She had heard of His teachings, but oh, how she longed in her heart to learn from Him. To listen to His voice meant hearing the very words of God.

What would He teach? Would He tell of miracles? Of Heaven?

Martha surely kept interrupting Mary's time of prayer and thoughts with commands to fetch more items from the market or straighten the table. Martha begged her sister to get her head out of the clouds and do what was needed. After all, it must be perfect for Jesus.

Mary could see a crowd building near the gates of the city; He must be here. Martha pressed her dress, brushed back her hair, took a deep breath and walked to the door. As He passed by, Martha requested Jesus and His disciples to come into her home and rest at their table.

"Now as they went on their way, Jesus entered a village. And a woman named Martha welcomed him into her house. And she had a sister called Mary, who sat at the Lord's feet and listened to his teaching" (Luke 10:38-39).

No sooner than Martha showed Jesus to the mat she had chosen on the floor, Mary would have sat directly at His feet. Her heart was so eager, I imagine she fought back the tears of joy. How she must have longed to hear His words. At that moment, nothing else mattered.

Despite all the benefits Mary saw at the feet of Jesus, Martha didn't, but rather let busyness and perfection keep her from resting and listening to Him.

The words of Jesus, the One who came to save sinners, were indescribable. He used this opportunity to be about the Father's business, sharing the love of God and salvation from sin. Mary was beyond words at all He said. But, Martha wasn't without words, and with a burning temper asked Jesus, "How could my sister leave me to this mess myself? How could she leave me with this load to bare alone? Does she not see how hard I am working, yet she offers me no help!"

"But, Martha was distracted with much serving. And she went up to him and said, "Lord, do you not care that my sister has left me to serve alone? Tell her then to help me" (Luke 10:40).

The role and place of a woman was apparent in their culture. There was no question to Martha that the place for her was not in the company of men where Mary was. But, to Mary it didn't matter - this was Jesus. Martha was fed up and took her case straight to Him. She was so distracted by the perfection she sought that she missed the importance of what was indeed taking place in her home.

The eyes of the room turned to Jesus as her question hung heavy in the air. Mary's eyes were wide when suddenly, Christ spoke with a gentle rebuke, "Martha, Martha, you are worried and upset about many things, but one thing is necessary." The rebuke of Christ stung in her chest, had she been so busy and distracted she failed to see what was important? Jesus continued, "Mary has made the right choice, and it will not be taken away from her" (Luke 10:41-42, CSB).

Mary had chosen what was right? How did she choose what was right when Martha had been working so hard to make things perfect for Jesus? Why wasn't He praising her for a job well done? Martha stood at the door, hurt from the rebuke, and watched her sister. Mary was taking in every word of Jesus. She wasn't concerned over the things that had Martha in a tizzy. She had chosen Jesus over striving to make things perfect.

It's Not Just Martha

Mary's attention wasn't the same as her sister's. Her focus was on Jesus, and her heart was unconcerned with the things around her that didn't matter - things she knew could wait. Her hunger to be near Him was greater than her desire to perform for Him.

Mary sat on the dusty floor at Jesus' feet, the One who came to be her Rescuer. She longed to learn from every word that poured from His mouth because He was God made flesh. She saw no need for the rush of works the way her sister Martha did. Mary only saw the benefit of learning from the Master.

I want to think Martha got it together in the end. The downfall of living like a Pharisee is following every letter to perfection, which isn't what Christ is after. He is after your heart.

[The Pharisees followed every letter of the law with no grace, and in all their striving they were fooled into believing their works were enough.]

Martha's constant striving left her with a bitter heart toward her sister, but more than that it left her missing out on the chance to soak up the words of Christ. Martha's tasks were not wrong, but they distracted her from the salvation she needed.

Jesus sought to redeem Martha from the burden of perfection and the weight that comes with a works-based faith.

Jesus told Martha her sister had chosen what was right. Being at His feet was freedom from striving. More often than not we find ourselves being more of a Martha than a Mary when we seek perfection instead of Jesus. What if we stopped treating our time with Jesus like Martha did, distracted by to do lists or chores and rushed for time because other things appear more important, and approached it like Mary, letting everything else wait while we sit at Jesus' feet and draw from His words. Jesus doesn't desire or require a performance or perfection. He only wants our time and devotion.

He came to redeem us from the trappings of this world - endless striving, demanding perfection, and the need to do it all. He offers us His grace and beckons our hearts, "Sit at my feet, let me refresh and restore your heart, and give peace to the thoughts that have you hurried and burdened."

"Come to me, all who labor and are heavy laden, and I will give you rest. Take my yoke upon you, and learn from me, for I am gentle and lowly in heart, and you will find rest for your souls" (Matthew 11:28-29).

I love the wording of this verse in the Message.

"Are you tired? Worn out? Burned out on religion? Come to me. Get away with me and you'll recover your life. I'll show you how to take a real rest. Walk with me and work with me - watch how I do it. Learn the unforced rhythms of grace. I won't lay anything heavy or ill-fitting on you. Keep company with me and you'll learn to live freely and lightly" (Matthew 11:28-29, MSG).

Our lives without grace are a mess. We don't deserve it, and that's what makes it beautiful. We cannot perform for it or attain it by the works of our hands. Grace is given, not taken. Grace cures us of our unrealistic expectations and ushers us to the feet of the Father in all things.

Jesus offers grace and reformation from our need to do it all. He pours out mercy when our striving gets the best of us. God reminds us who we are in Him when we find ourselves comparing our lives to the women around us. We don't need perfection because He is our Perfecter and all we need.

God doesn't demand our striving, so we shouldn't require it of ourselves. The hours spent believing we have to get it all right and do it all to find value in the eyes of Christ is false.

Martha had to learn that no amount of works she accomplished would make God love her more. She was so wrapped up in the work of impressing the Messiah she missed the very reason why He came.

He wants our weakness, our mess, and our deep-seated fears. He wants to display His perfect power in us and turn our lives into a walking message of the gospel.

The Messes We Cannot Control

Life will throw messes at us that we have no control over, but God is faithful to meet us in our deepest hurts.

CHAPTER FIVE
The Mess of Grief

Naomi (Ruth 1:9-22)

As a little girl, I would sit on my daddy's lap and make him promise he would live forever. There is something in the innocence of a child who doesn't yet see the mortality of life, the brevity that weighs heavy over each one of us. My sweet daddy would look at me with his deep brown eyes, smile, and kiss my face. He never promised because he knew it was an impossible request. I was twenty-one when every childhood dream I had of my father living forever was ripped away.

That day won't leave my memory. It will always be there tucked away like a thorn digging into my flesh. There is no escaping the memories; trying to reach him on the phone, hearing about ambulances, hospitals, head scans and reports of a massive brain aneurysm. The outcome was grim, and my heart would never be the same.

My brother and I took the first flight we could. As the wheels of the plane hit the ground, a voicemail shattered everything I knew into a million pieces. We were too late. He was gone.

Walking into the hospital at 2:00 a.m. we saw the halls were empty and an unsettled silence filled the air. I just needed to see him, to touch him. The tears fell heavy down my face as I held his hand and kissed his face. My daddy, the one I knew could conquer the world, was gone.

Death can be unbearably cruel to those left behind.

Devastated doesn't even begin to scratch the surface of the depth of emotion I went through. Grief ravaged my heart and mind and turned my entire world upside down.

The morning after my father passed I lay in a hotel room, staring at the ceiling. Without warning I had lost my best friend. I couldn't sleep, I couldn't pray, I couldn't breathe. I felt I had been cheated of time I so desperately wanted.

Thinking of those moments now...my eyes again fill with tears, as if the sting of grief were still fresh. It was as if I was standing still, unable to move while the world kept spinning. I couldn't understand why life kept its hustling pace while I remained paralyzed.

The harrowing effects of grief aren't just over the lives lost, but the stolen moments we cannot reclaim. We grieve what we cannot have. Parents shouldn't have to bury children, and young children shouldn't have to bury their parents. There are lifetimes of memories with my dad that my family will never get to make and treasure - moments of laughter and silliness with my children, sharing writing accomplishments with him that I know he would have been embarrassingly proud of, and even phone calls throughout the day to share daily life.

I learned something incredibly valuable in what would turn out to be the first of many devastating losses in my life; God didn't fail me. He didn't abandon me there in my moment of need, and He won't ever leave me in my desperate situations. This place of heartache was not without purpose in the Kingdom of God.

"God is our refuge and strength, a very present help in trouble" (Psalm 46:1).

Refuge in Grief

"In the days when the judges ruled there was a famine in the land, and a man of Bethlehem in Judah went to sojourn in the country of Moab, he and his wife and his two sons" (Ruth 1:1).

Israel was no stranger to the turmoil of famines, wars, and times of desperation. The "house of bread" (Bethlehem) could no longer feed its families. When Naomi looked out over her barren garden and saw that the crops and food they stored had finally run out, she must have felt she had no choice but to leave.

Her husband Elimelech and their two sons, Mahlon and Chilion, packed what they could. They took only the precious things they could carry because the journey would be long. They needed food to survive, and it was no longer found in Bethlehem. Their desperation drove them from all that was familiar; they were now refugees looking for a new home in the unknown, searching for a place of hope.

Their feet kicked up dust along the way, but it did not diminish their spirit. I imagine Naomi turned to her husband with a look in her eyes that begged the question, "Where will we call home?"

Moab was a neighboring city, but what would it cost them to settle in this place? The Israelites once spent years in the land of Moab before they entered the land of Canaan. The history between them held a past of hatred and hostility (Numbers 22-25). Ultimately, her family's desperate search for food brought them from the "house of bread" to this place of uncertainty.

The years passed in this foreign country, and gradually this land became their home. Naomi began to see a glimmer of hope on the horizon, that was, until the morning it all changed. Hope was snatched out from under her feet - her beloved husband was gone without warning. She was left all alone in a foreign land with her two sons and their wives (Ruth 1:3-4).

She had lost her home and the land she loved, and now this. Elimelech was the reason they were here, he had chosen this place for his family, and now she was on her own. Despite her heartache, she was not unseen. God, after all, is El-Roi the God who sees, and He saw Naomi in her grief.

Soon Naomi would bury both sons next to their father. How incredibly cruel it must have felt to lose it all. The divide between Naomi and God felt so wide, the anger too great, and it all became too much. She wondered how God could rip away all that she loved from her hands. Losing her husband was horrible, but losing both of her sons was unimaginable. For years Naomi had prayed over them, their wives, and their future children. Now they were gone along with all her most precious dreams.

There was no hope left in this land that was foreign to her. There was no life left within the walls of her home. The comfort of Bethlehem beckoned her; her people held what little hope she had left.

She sat there with grieving daughters-in-law on either side, Orpah and Ruth, two Moabite women. They both had waited so long for families of their own, only for it not to come.

Ruth had come to know of Jehovah from this family who didn't worship manufactured idols but a living and powerful God. She heard the stories of His incredible power; the great I AM who parted the sea and gathered with His people by cloud and fire in the wilderness. No idol had ever accomplished such incredible feats as the Almighty God of Israel.

Ruth stuck by Naomi, who was not just her mother-in-law, but her spiritual mother as well. Naomi took care to tell her daughters-in-law about Jehovah God. Ruth knew Bethlehem would be her home if that's where she could be with Naomi and know more of God.

"But Ruth said, "Do not urge me to leave you or to return from following you. For where you go I will go, and where you lodge I will lodge. Your people shall be my people, and your God my God" (Ruth 1:16).

Naomi and Ruth shared common grief. God had brought them both into barrenness and overwhelming pain to reveal the heart of who He was, and what He had for both of them. Naomi couldn't see it yet, because her heart was still overcome with bitterness for all she had walked. Naomi returned to Bethlehem with a new name - Mara, which means bitterness.

She and Ruth stepped forward together, into the unknown of their future. Naomi would see God again and the beauty of His plan.

The God who saw her, El-Roi.

Jehovah-Jireh, the Lord who provided all for her.

Jehovah-Shammah, the Lord who was there even in her despair.

Jehovah-Rapha, the Lord who would heal her broken heart.

Jehovah-Shalom, the Lord who is peace, though she felt none.

Jehovah-Rapha: The Lord Who Heals

Grief is cruel and leaves you walking into an unknown future, alone. Losing my dad became desperately hard in the moments I wanted to share with him. The grief came in what I could not have as a daughter. There were no phone calls about my children, no crying together over things that hurt, and there will be no celebration with him when I hold this finished book in my hands.

Losing my earthly father led me into the arms of my Heavenly Father. No longer could this daddy's girl rely on a dad to be on the other end of a phone call or receive a hug that engulfed my entire body. I needed my Abba, my Daddy God, who comforts, loves, and treasures me.

Grief can thrust us into the arms of the Father.

2 Corinthians 1:3-5 says this of God, "Blessed be the God and the Father of our Lord Jesus Christ, the Father of mercies and the God of all comfort, who comforts us in all our affliction, so that we may be able to comfort those who are in any affliction, with the comfort with which we ourselves are comforted by God. For as we share abundantly in Christ's sufferings, so through Christ we share abundantly in comfort too."

God is a God of comfort; He is Jehovah Rapha - the God who heals.

Comfort comes in the grief; it doesn't discolor the pain, but it offers the peace that transcends any words I attempt to put on a page. Naomi found comfort in returning home, coming back to what she knew to be true - her God. She still wore the bitterness of grief, but she sought the only thing that could heal her broken heart. With comfort, over time comes healing. True healing from the pain of grief can only come from God.

In Him we survive grief because He is our Comfort and Healer.

In Him we survive grief because He is our Comfort and Healer.

Grief requires comfort, but it also requires faith. The faith that He is still good regardless of our circumstances. He won't leave our side even when the lonely ache of sadness pierces our heart, and despite our feelings, it doesn't have to dictate our worship.

Comfort in death comes with the hope of resurrection.

1 Thessalonians 4:13-18 reminds us, "But we do not want you to be uninformed, brother, about those who are asleep, that you may not grieve as others do who have no hope. For since we believe that Jesus died and rose again, even so, through Jesus, God will bring with him those who have fallen asleep. For this we declare to you by a word from the Lord, that we who are alive, who are left until the coming for the Lord, will not precede those who have fallen asleep. For the Lord himself will descend from heaven with a cry of command, with the voice of an archangel, and with the sound of the trumpet of God. And the dead in Christ will rise first. Then we who are alive, who are left, will be caught up together with them in the clouds to meet the Lord in the air, and so we will always be with the Lord. Therefore, encourage one another with these words."

Grieving without hope is anguish to the soul, but grieving with the promise of Christ brings life to our most profound pain.

Naomi wasn't left to grieve alone, she wasn't left to mourn without hope. God brought comfort in the form of a baby through her daughter-in-law Ruth, who would become a part of the line of David, the line that led to the King of all Kings. Jesus. Her grief was redeemed with joy, with great and abundant hope in the One who would conquer death and the grave. The One who would take our sin to a cross and destroy the holds of death and deliver us into eternity. There is no greater hope.

"He will wipe away every tear from their eyes, and death shall be no more, neither shall there be mourning, nor crying, nor pain anymore, for the former things have passed away" (Revelation 21:4).

The vapor that is our life holds no flame to the boundless eternity of heaven. No sorrow or pain will be welcome on those golden streets. The magnificent power of God will wipe every tear away once and for all, and the bondage of grief will no longer hold us when we are present with Jesus. This life is limited, but eternity is without end.

The mess of grief is inevitable; it will rock our worlds, if it hasn't already. But, there is comfort and healing for the pain we face. Holy Mess isn't just the messes we make but, also these unavoidable places of life on this earth where God meets us in each unbearable moment and shows up with the gospel every time.

CHAPTER SIX
The Mess of Rejection
Leah (Genesis 29-30)

I wish there was some way to pour something sweet or funny over these things we cannot control - these messes that feel unfairly given to us.

Rejection is one of them. I could tell you all my stories of being rejected, and I am sure you could tell me yours - all the hurts and utter devastation that come with this one little word. But, some stories aren't for me to tell. Some stories are for us to have with God alone.

We all deal with deep down, tucked-in wounds. Ones we cover with masks of all kinds to keep them out of reach of our emotions and thoughts. But, they are there, and they will eventually rise to the surface.

The actions or inactions of others can shape us at our core. Their rejection can be carried for decades, and weasel its way into our relationships with others. But, more than that, it can drive a wedge between God and us if we let it.

We cannot let the rejection others give steer the direction of our hearts.

Rejection is a hard pill to swallow and leaves wounds we want no one else to see. We fight to keep hidden the bruises of feeling discarded. Often, these greatest hurts come from those we trust the most.

We cannot let the rejection others give steer the direction of our hearts.

Rejection stole more than my worth; it robbed me of relationships.

Being rejected is often the result of someone else's choice; it's a wound that can be inflicted unknowingly or with purpose. It's more than a flesh wound, yes, it is much deeper than that. The gashes it leaves behind need more than a band-aid to heal.

If we hinder these wounds from being brushed off, they begin to cripple us from the inside out. Within us they breed the lie that we are not loved, wanted, or valued. Hurts like this don't just vanish in a moment with one prayer. They become like stitched up surgical cuts plagued with scars, hardened and calloused, that keep healthy skin from growing in their place. While all seems fine on the outside, the images of our insides would reveal the trauma, scar tissue, and internal bleeding caused by external emotional wounds.

This kind of damage conceives an identity wrapped up in pain, which gives way to deceptions of the enemy. The thing about rejection is that the lie it births creates a desperation to fill a massive void, an emptiness most of us believe God cannot fix, or we don't trust Him enough to let Him heal.

Rejection requires God's touch, and we need to see how God uses it to the praise of His glory.

Marked as Unwanted

Despite being the oldest daughter of Laban, Leah was a timid girl with "weak eyes" (Genesis 29:17) and she spent her life trying to live up to her younger sister Rachel. Rachel was beautiful, charming, and seemed to be the joy of her father, far more than Leah ever would. She lived her life in the shadows, while her sister received all the attention.

In their culture, there was great shame in being the oldest daughter and still unmarried; the young men in the town wouldn't even give her a second glance, but they never failed to notice Rachel.

Jacob, Laban's nephew by his sister Sarai, came back to his mother's family in search of a wife and without surprise, Rachel caught his eye. Surely Leah couldn't hide the heat that radiated from her face with the news that he wanted to marry the youngest rather than the oldest daughter. (Just something else to add to her list – not beautiful enough and now unwanted). Nothing about this life she had been handed felt fair even though she was faithful to God and loyal to her father.

She knew about the passionate moment Rachel and Jacob shared at the well when he first came into the village. How she longed to be loved that way, loved in a way that made her feel safe and whole.

Jacob waited seven years for Rachel's hand. Leah was hopeful she would be married before her sister's wedding and she held out hope God would bring the perfect man for her. Those seven years may have felt like mere days for Jacob and Rachel, but for Leah, it felt like heartbreak day after day. No one wanted her the way Jacob wanted Rachel.

"So Laban gathered together all the people of the place and made a feast. But in the evening he took his daughter Leah and brought her to Jacob, and he went in to her" (Genesis 29:22-23).

There are so many unknown details about this story. Did Leah know her father's plan? Did she go willingly? While we wonder about the details, the facts are what stand. When Jacob woke up, he wasn't married to the woman he wanted. Nothing speaks rejection to our hearts more than being unwanted.

When Jacob realized what Laban had done, it was too late. They were married, and Jacob was overcome with anger; Leah was not who he wanted. She found herself rejected and despised within hours of being married. I wonder if she heard the fight between Jacob and her father, "I didn't want her as my wife, I wanted Rachel, and you tricked me into taking her." Laban must have fought back, "You may not have wanted her, but she is yours now." Then, to hear another deal made for Jacob to marry Rachel. Anguish and defeat must have filled her heart. Now she was to share her husband with the sister she had lived in the shadow of all her life.

All Leah had left was God; the only hope of being seen and wanted rested solely in the Father. God saw how much Leah was hated and He had compassion on her. He allowed her to have children but closed the womb of her sister Rachel.

"When the LORD saw that Leah was hated, he opened her womb, but Rachel was barren" (Genesis 29:31).

The names of Leah's children became a reflection of what God was unfolding in this woman's heart.

She gave birth to a son, Reuben whose name meant "the Lord has seen my affliction; for now my husband will love me."

Simeon, because "the Lord heard I was hated he gave me a son also."

Levi, because "Now this time my husband will be attached to me, because I have borne him three sons."

Each son, to her, was a way to win the heart of her husband, but God was doing something different; He was revealing Himself to this woman who needed to be rescued from the burden she carried. We see it when she gives Judah his name, "this time I will praise the Lord" (Genesis 29:31-35).

God desired to use her life for something greater. He was faithful to see her and love her when her family saw her as unlovable and discarded.

Rejected, But Not Unseen

The pain of rejection leaves us without security, giving into every fear, doubt, and disbelief that plagues our bones. For me, every ounce of pain in my life became a threat; the many rejections over the years culminated in the beginning of my undoing.

I allowed the perception of rejection in my life to keep me stuck in a pattern of self-destruction. My destructive path sought out relationships that gave the temporary illusion of security. I sought to mend my broken heart by placing it in the hands of those who had no power to fix it, and they often left it more fractured than they found it.

But God says, "He will bind up the brokenhearted and bind up their wounds" (Psalm 147:3).

Stick with me…

I chose to believe the worst in those who hurt me rather than letting go. Hurts we receive as a child are not easily mended, and without Jesus, we can spend decades seeking wholeness. But, with God there is hope for the unwanted, there is peace in the midst of piercing pain, and there is healing from the mess left behind.

He reaches out His hand to us and begins to pull at the threads of our deepest hurts and rejections until it slowly begins to unravel into His hands. God will not leave us in this place, this place where we long to fill holes and gaps others leave behind. God unravels us, all the while mending us with His perfect grace.

Grace is enough for every rejection and heartache.

Grace is enough for every rejection and heartache.

God saw Leah rejected by her husband and unloved by her sister. Each one of her children became a reminder that God knew her and loved her. Each name they bore marked what God had done in her life. She believed if she gave Jacob the sons he desired, then he would finally love her the way he loved Rachel. She began to learn a beautiful truth - it wasn't Jacob's love for her that mattered, but God's love that mattered above all.

Leah needed to see her situation through the eyes of the Father.

She was left unwanted by the world, but not unseen by God.

The mess of rejection robs us of the ability to see how God sees.

It became more important how God saw her than how others saw her, or even how she saw herself.

God met me in my worst moments. My Heavenly Father filled the holes left by others and He alone changed my heart that felt hated and undesirable. He spoke truth to a teen girl that carried this weight and offered her freedom from the burden it caused. Most who have experienced rejection know it can leave us with gaps in our hearts, holes in the shape of a wooden cross that can only be filled by grace.

Rejection is contradictory to the gospel which says you are wholly loved and chosen. Our hurts can blind us to the truth that God loves us so much He willingly sacrificed His Son on our behalf. Our hearts may be wrecked by the actions of others, but they don't stand a chance against the power of the cross.

There is grace for the rejected and forgotten. Hebrews 4:15 reminds us, "For we do not have a high priest who is unable to sympathize with our weaknesses, but one who in every respect has been tempted as we are, yet without sin." Gracious and merciful Jesus was rejected by His chosen people and His beautiful creation all the way to the cross.

Psalm 118:22, "The stone that the builders rejected has become the cornerstone."

Luke 17:25, "But first he must suffer many things and be rejected by this generation."

God is faithful to see us in every brokenhearted circumstance. He is a loving Father who meets us in our rejection and reminds us we are truly loved. Our gracious God meets us in the heartbreak and gently fills the wounds of our hearts with His love.

In a world where we so often feel hidden, God sees.

In our lives when we feel battered by rejection, God gives His grace.

God will never reject us when we come to Him with hearts open unto salvation.

His love for us is greater than any rejection we could possibly face. He is ready to meet us in it and offer the healing only He can give.

CHAPTER SEVEN

The Mess of Waiting

Sarai (Genesis 16-17)

Waiting can feel like utter darkness. Uncertainty lurks ahead of you, and the unknowns of the future darken your way leaving you groping for the right path. Your stomach churns, and you are torn between what you selfishly want and what God seems to be doing.

There have been far too many of those seasons in my life. Sometimes I fall into the lie that I know better than the Father and my plan is better than His. It is in those moments I lunge for control and try to take action, not noticing the unstable step I am about to take could cause more harm.

Waiting hurts.

Waiting is messy.

Waiting wounds the control freak that lives within our flesh. It is against the grain of our nature to wait patiently, so it takes the rewiring of our brains by the Holy Spirit for us to walk in obedience with God.

I have experienced more than one season of intense waiting; waiting to get pregnant after two years of trying and brutal loss, waiting for the healing of loved ones I never saw fulfilled, and waiting as God called my family in a new direction with limited answers. These waiting

God puts us in torn tension to teach us there is no plan greater than His.

moments can feel as if the rest of the world is moving at an obscene speed while we are barely inching forward.

Waiting is an expectant action for all who face it. Expectant that soon God will fulfill His promise or give us the desire our heart aches for.

There is immense tension found in waiting; it is the raw place between what used to be and what is yet to come. It refines us like a fire down deep in our bones. God puts us in torn tension to teach us there is no plan greater than His.

Author Sarah Hagerty says it like this, "All the waiting rooms in life, the wasteful places where the only question is, "When will I ever get out of this place?" are the places God loves to show Himself."[3]

Our family was there again, in a new season of waiting for God to move and breathe answers into our confusion. It was as if when the clock struck midnight on the new year that God slowly began unraveling and revealing a new plan for us. God opened a new door for ministry we hadn't even considered and it was as though Isaiah 43:19 was being displayed in front of us. "Behold I am doing a new thing; now it springs forth, do you not perceive it? I will make a way in the wilderness and rivers in the desert."

This plan of Gods was shrouded in unknowns. We could only see the beginning, the very first steps of saying yes to Him. We felt as though God was pulling us from our most comfortable to our most vulnerable. This is where obedience requires open hands.

The most significant test for us in waiting is often revealed in the opening and closing of our hands. When our hands are tightly closed, even if we consider ourselves walking in obedience, God cannot place a blessing in them. We are unable to receive it. Our closed fists reveal our underlying desire to control. Open hands in the waiting is fully saying yes to God despite having to wait to see it through - it is letting go of that control-freak we all dislike in ourselves.

Even if we had all the information, would we obey God? In the Old Testament, the wilderness came with evident, audible promises from God to His children. They were given the details, they knew the end result, yet they chose to disobey God. They chose complaining and idols over God and the promised land.

Waiting seasons will test how much we actually trust God and the sovereign plan He has for us, despite not knowing all the details.

Open hands in the waiting is fully saying yes to God despite having to wait to see it through.

Barren and Broken

Everything looked uncertain. Life as she had known it was over. Now there was only an uncertain future. Her husband, Abram, had been called by God to a great promise, one she couldn't fathom as she placed her hand over her empty womb. Her husband would become the father of a great nation who would settle in a land of God's choosing.

Kings would arise from his lineage, and his name would be known for generations.

Sarai surely must have wondered how God would make a great nation from her husband when she could not bear children. How could God promise something she was unable to give? The weight of the promise lingered heavy in the air and in their tent at night. Sarai, a wife who longed for nothing more than to have children, grieved in the waiting season where God had placed her.

Abram and his beloved wife's journey to the promised land proved long, with hot sand under their feet during the day and stars overhead as they camped at night. But faithfully, God met with Abram, showing him the fullness of what his descendants would receive.

I wonder if with every step of their journey Sarai grew more and more bitter toward the promises of God. This promise that in her own eyes didn't include a barren woman. The grief of her empty womb inflamed her pride as the incessant waiting began to take its toll. Unknowingly to Sarai, her impatient heart would have to wait twenty-five years before seeing the promise of holding her child come to fruition. A child she believed impossible.

Abram was a man of promise with a barren wife. What looked like a hopeless or unfulfilled promise to Sarai, was a plan being fulfilled on schedule by God. Sarai learned what we all learn at some point in our lives, "For my thoughts are not your thoughts, neither are your ways my ways, declare the Lord" (Isaiah 55:8).

Sarai wrung her hands and paced the floor as she began to reason through her situation. Her heart's desire was to give her husband a son, so surely, it would be in God's will to allow Abram to conceive a child with Hagar, her handmaid. After all, it wasn't an uncommon practice for barren women in their culture. She justified sinful disobedience with cultural standards.

Regretfully, Hagar conceived more than just a son; her pregnancy also birthed bitterness and anger. Sarai's plan had backfired. Ishmael should have been her child; she should have been the one to carry a son for her husband. It quickly revealed her impatience and gave birth to sin. Sarai had taken matters into her own hands out of selfishness, pride, and impatience. Her plan left her crushed and in a horrible mess.

Girl, Stop Overthinking It

I also have spent seasons waiting and wondering. It is during these times when we are forced to be still that we fail to see God is always moving. We long for quick answers, perfect outcomes, and solutions that fit within our desires.

We overthink it at the best of times and crumble under the weight at the worst of times.

It is in the hidden seasons God teaches us waiting is holy business.

When God called our family to a new church, to a ministry role for my husband, there was so much in us that resisted. How would this turn out? What did God want from our family? How would we survive in a new place? Our questions came with silent answers and anguish as we wrestled for every step forward. We had been in far worse situations than this, but this felt like an earth-shaking move of God in our family. It's in seasons when

It is in the hidden seasons God teaches us waiting is holy business.

God asks us to wait that He refines our heart to receive a greater blessing beyond our place of desperation.

We were desperate for answers - we, in our flesh, wanted to know what God was doing in the midst. It wasn't until we were still enough to listen that God began dealing strongly with us. It wasn't until we realized that this was about God's plan and not our own, and began reconciling ourselves to the sovereignty of our Heavenly Father, that we found peace - even in the struggle of letting go of our comfort zone and our security.

I waited.

I prayed.

I wept.

All the while, God saw me.

It was in that season God taught me His plans were far better than any I could create for myself. God would use every moment for His glory. He would use every ounce of how He broke us for His glory and our benefit. You see, God's plan was indeed perfect, because He gave us a calling and complete peace, in His time. And in the waiting, He gave me an even better gift, the gift of fully trusting in Him.

If we never have seasons of waiting, we miss the benefit of growing.

If we never have seasons of waiting, we miss the benefit of growing.

It is tempting in the darkness of waiting to seek out light, grabbing for any lifeline we can find or attempting to make our own solutions. Unfortunately, most of them are not in God's plan. Sarai longed to witness the

86

promise of God fulfilled, to hold her baby in her hands. In her impatience, rather than allowing God to light the way, she sought to make her own at the expense of her husband and her servant.

The reason waiting is messy is because we make it that way. It becomes a disaster when we get restless in the waiting and long to control our situations by taking things into our own hands. It's at that moment we begin inventing our own light.

Our impatience can cause dangerous detours.

Friend, stay in your lane and remain steadfast in the waiting because redemption is coming. The promise ahead will be fulfilled, and He will reveal the light.

Prolific writer Oswald Chambers says this, "Genesis 16 is an example of listening to so-called good advice during a time of darkness, rather than waiting for God to send the light. When God gives you a vision and darkness follows, wait. God will bring the vision he has given you to reality in your life if you will wait on his timing. Never try to help God fulfill his word."[4]

Sarai's advice to Abram was not part of the original plan, but the impatience found in waiting added a layer of mess to an already uncertain season. Hagar became a part of the equation because Sarai wouldn't be obedient in the stillness.

When we cannot accept the tension that lies in the middle of waiting we will make a mess of things. We will jump ahead of God's plan and miss what He has set for us. The lesson of her story is that if we jump ahead of God, it will not end up all rainbows and sunshine. Her impatience led to enormous consequences, but God by grace alone still allowed her to be a part of His promise.

Sarai believed what the culture around her told her – barren women were cursed by God. The waiting brought about an impatience in her that was a dangerous mixture of pride and bitterness. Offering her servant to her husband was not unheard of in her culture; in fact, it was common. Any child born from that union did not belong to the servant but to her mistress and would stand as her child. We come to find this arrangement didn't work in the case of Sarai and Ishmael. Hagar's conception only conceived resentment.

God didn't exclude Sarai from the covenant. He saw Sarai despite her impatience and abuse of Hagar and restored her fully. God, who can turn a mess into something for His glory, allowed Sarai to become Sarah, the mother of nations and kings, and the only woman in Scripture to receive a sacramental name (a name given by God).

Wow – let me pump the breaks to say this...

Don't get disillusioned to think your sin will work out.

It won't.

The damage will be done.

But God will get His glory, and God will always keep His promise.

Her name held weight under the promise that God had given to Abraham because her task required a name that fit her purpose.

"God said to Abraham, "As for your wife Sarai, do not call her Sarai, for Sarah will be her name. I will bless her; indeed, I will give you a son by her. I will bless her, and she will produce nations; kings of peoples will come from her" (Genesis 17:15-16, CSB).

God did not leave Sarah unseen in her waiting; He set her apart to be the mother of nations and the matriarch of kings. She was an important factor in the promises of God; her womb would be full, and what was once barren, would thrive. Her longings would be fulfilled just as God said they would. Her son, Isaac, would father Jacob, who would father the twelve tribes of Israel, whose lineage continues today. What favor of God! What redemption of a woman who was called to a season of waiting.

God revealed a light for Sarah in her darkness, and He will reveal light to us. We don't have to be at a standstill in our season of waiting. Leaning into His promises and standing on the truth of God's Word will reveal direction and purpose when we find ourselves grappling with the unknown.

Our God is a God of His Word. The Word defined by pages held in our hands, and a Son, the Word made flesh, who would take up the cross and defeat death. The Word that whispered the world into existence and life into the lungs of man. That same Word is our God, our Redeemer, and the One who calls us His holy daughters.

The Messes God Makes in Us

God makes a beautiful mess in our lives through the process of sanctification. We can do nothing to earn our salvation, but we get to be active participants in the process of growing and becoming more like Christ.

CHAPTER EIGHT
The Mess of Courage
Esther (Esther 1-8)

The truth - I am the girl who is afraid of everything. I am thirty-two and cannot sleep without some sort of light on. Fear and anxiety have been a thorn in my flesh for as long as I can remember. I fear things most "normal" people don't even think about. I am the girl who assumes a tumor at the first sign of pain and the mom who dwells on every worst-case scenario.

I'm far more comfortable hiding in my bubble at home. That's the trap of fear; it will keep us from saying yes to God and taking steps in obedience.

Fear is never from God.

"For God did not give us a spirit of timidity or cowardice or fear, but {He has given us a spirit} of power and of love and of sound judgment and personal discipline {abilities that result in a calm, well-balanced mind and self-control}" (2 Timothy 1:7, AMP).

So much to my amazement, God called this scared, anxiety-plagued girl to do something that was far out of her comfort zone. I was sure (and sometimes still wonder if) God was playing some kind of joke.

Needless to say, my first time speaking to a crowd of women about Jesus didn't quite start as I had hoped.

I found myself crouched against the wall in the dark hallway, my mind swirling with doubts, and my heart beating as if I was suddenly in survival mode. God and I had talked about this. I told Him I was not a speaker. I would write, but I drew the line at speaking. I believed no one in the world wanted to hear anything that came out of my mouth and that my awkwardness would be too much for the world to bear.

Nonetheless, there I was on the other side of a room filling with women and I needed to find whatever it was going to take to get me to turn on the microphone and speak.

When I told God my thoughts on speaking, He laughed and gave a quick, "Watch me." You would think at this point in my relationship with Him I would have learned saying "never" to Him was a horrible idea.

I was scared out of my mind, like pass-the-brown-paper-bag-so-I-can-breathe-heavily-into-it kind of scared. I wanted nothing more than to bolt for the nearest exit. The door looked better than being vulnerable and teaching hard truths.

I had become content staying hidden, quietly seeking God without all eyes on me. He had begun this very intricate refining process in me, and I see now His purpose was bigger than what I desired for myself. I didn't know opening the Word would become the key to a calling, a command to step out from my mess.

The call to obedience, in reality, eliminated the exit as an option. We only anticipated maybe ten women to attend this event, but suddenly it became a room of fifty-five. My strength failed me. My courage was long gone with my initial thoughts of escape. I felt crippled with panic. I whispered under my breath, "This is not the place for me," as if reminding Him of my weakness would change His mind. At that moment a fresh voice fell upon my heart, "Just begin."

God offers His Holy Spirit in the simple act of our saying yes to His call. The words came slowly and cracked under the weight of my nervous voice, but the one simple step forward required I take ahold of spiritual courage. I needed His strength in the midst of what I believed to be my greatest weakness. When I finished what felt like an impossible task, I knew it was all God.

He crafts the spiritual courage it takes to serve Him. It is not a result of our ability. If it all relied on our efforts and strength, there would be no need for God. If it were dependent on us, God would select only the qualified for great Kingdom tasks. For a writer and teacher, He would be required to choose only those with degrees and accolades to their name, not a woman who has never set foot on a seminary campus and struggles with sentence structure and misspelled words. (Yep, that's me.)

If spiritual courage relied on qualifications, many of Scripture's biggest names would have never been given a chance.

God doesn't call those who are equipped for the task. He equips the ones He calls.

Moses would have never been able to aid the rescue of God's chosen people.

Gideon would have remained hidden.

Joseph would never have forgiven the brothers who wanted him dead.

Paul would have remained Saul.

Rahab would have remained in her desolate life of prostitution.

The list could go on for pages. God doesn't call those who are equipped for the task. He equips the ones He calls. Ephesians 2:8-10, "For you are saved by grace through faith, and this is not from yourselves; it is

God's gift - not from works so that no one can boast. For we are his workmanship, created in Christ Jesus for good works, which God prepared ahead of time for us to do."

Beautiful Courage

Esther was an intense beauty with something about her that was unlike all of the other girls her age. The death of her parents had left a story hidden behind her dark eyes. The only way of life she had ever known was born from captivity when her family became exiles. Even with the option of release from this place that marked their capture, her family stayed; the Persian Empire was their home. Their captivity had become their security.

After decades of living in a pagan land, their religion had become unrecognizable. Esther likely kept her faith hidden because that is what she had been taught all of her life. Revealing her Jewish heritage would have made her a target; unveiling her God could very well have meant death.

Esther was in the care of her cousin, Mordecai, who raised her as his daughter, teaching her to be faithful to God. All of this teaching was with purpose and God-ordained because she would soon need it.

King Ahasuerus had removed the queen and was in search of a new bride to take her place. He wasn't looking for just anyone. Beautiful virgins were what he desired and Esther, like every girl in the empire, knew the king always got what he wanted.

The girls who met the king's requirements were gathered up to be taken to the palace. I am sure there was no choice for the women he wanted. The officials took one look at Esther and knew she would be just what the king would like.

Mordecai, being an official of the king, warned her of what she was to expect in this new life in the king's palace. The fear welled up in her heart as she thought, "Is this now my new captivity? Captive to a king?" She knew if the king didn't choose her, her fate was sealed to live her life as a concubine. This wasn't what she had envisioned for herself. Without choice, this was her new life.

A year of preparation marked the beginning of her time in the harem. Beauty treatments, new clothes, and all the jewelry one could imagine were at her disposal. She could have had anything she wanted before she was presented to the king, but this simple Jewish girl only asked for what her handler recommended. She knew this was not a princess party or dress up because Mordecai had explained what was expected when she went before the king. In essence, Esther was chosen for the king's beauty pageant to satisfy his grotesque lust and pride.

This 'new' captivity saw her being a possession rather than a valued treasure.

I imagine Esther trembled as she stood outside the king's door, her heart filled with fear as she breathed a prayer heavenward for courage and favor. This girl who should have been disqualified by law because of her nationality, found favor with the king. King Ahasuerus chose her to be his queen and placed the royal crown upon her head.

Esther found herself queen of the Persian Empire, one hundred and twenty-seven provinces resting under the scepter of her husband. Esther believed the hard days of the harem were behind her. This new role was one she never wanted, but somehow it was the one she had been given. Ahead of her lay a life of ease and comfort.

What could go wrong?

Esther was reclining with her maidens at the palace when her servant brought word from Mordecai. He bent low to whisper the message from her cousin, and her eyes trembled under the weight of fear. Haman, second in command to the king, had devised a plan to kill all of the Jews in the Empire without just cause or provocation. Since her first day at the palace, Esther had kept her nationality hidden out of fear, and at this moment she was reminded why.

She was the only one in a position to affect change; the only one who could plead the Jew's case before the king. Mordecai's reminder to her echos through history, "...and who knows whether you have not come to the kingdom for such a time as this?" (Esther 4:14). This pivotal moment of decision for Esther would determine the survival of the Jews from genocide and destruction.

God placed her within the palace walls for such a time as this.

God allowed her to be chosen for such a time as this.

God made her queen for such a time as this.

Esther knew going before the king could very well mean her life because no one appeared before him without being called. The fear overwhelmed her, but God, who had faithfully walked with her people for generations, gave her courage. If she died before the king, she would die trying to save her people. Her plea was the least she could do.

Take Heart

As a mom of three kids, I feel utterly ordinary, and I like it that way. I love the feeling of being hidden behind peanut butter and jelly sandwiches, and stacks of homeschool books on my kitchen table. To me, my children are my most precious calling, far above writing and speaking to women.

I never thought being a wife and mother would be a job God would offer me or even one I wanted. There is incredible spiritual courage needed to be a godly mother, facing every day, and the weight that comes with raising tiny humans for Jesus. I have to take hold of the gospel every second when the coffee is cold, and the children are loud, just as much as it is needed when I stand on a stage to speak.

Courage isn't limited just to the strong, and it is not limited merely to the weak. It is not just for the mothers, wives, or women in ministry. It is for you, the one waiting tables to feed her family, the woman behind a desk working long hours, and the college girl searching to find her way. Spiritual courage is from God and available to all.

I can't manufacture courage; I am not brave enough.

I can't manifest it; I am not strong enough.

The Holy Spirit, however, can develop courage in us because He is brave enough.

His Spirit can raise us to our feet because He is strong enough.

Scripture reminds us again and again that courage is for the taking.

There is a specific type of courage talked about in Scripture over 250 times, a form of it is used in the Old Testament Hebrew, and it is usually used in the form of the phrase *take courage*. We do not take courage because of ourselves, but because of our hope in who God is, what He has done, and what He will do.

Ezra took courage because the hand of the Lord was on him (Ezra 7:28).

Azariah, son of Obed the prophet, took courage and destroyed idols (2 Chronicles 15:8).

Paul in Philippians 1:20 says, "As it is my eager expectation and hope that I will not be ashamed, but that with full courage now as always Christ will be honored in my body, whether by life or death." Paul's courage stemmed from his hope in Christ, as does mine.

In the middle of the messes we cannot control, but are allowed by God, courage finds its place. In between the grieving, rejection, and calling of God there lies the spiritual courage we need as a believer. We need His persevering courage in the defining and desperate moments when we have nothing left to bring to the fight.

Spiritual courage is grounded in God's strength.

Esther was an unlikely hero, a simple Jewish girl who found herself in the palace for such a time as this to save her people. God is a God of order, purpose, and high power, and her placement was no mistake. Ours isn't either. He knows us in a way that is greater than we can imagine or fathom in our finite minds. He is an infinite God who has a purpose for you and me.

His courage is for the taking in the moments when He summons us to glorify Him in new or hard places. His courage finds us and is offered freely. It is what keeps us going when we are called to lead, minister, or do holy work for God's kingdom. (Yes, that even includes changing diapers and kissing scrapes, because raising babies is sacred work!)

We have believed the lie that we can be enough by ourselves, but our courage will fail us. We are blind to the need that we are not enough apart from Christ. The battlefield of faith will crush us without spiritual courage from our Heavenly Father. We will fall short without being reminded daily that it's not us but God who supplies our need.

Being called to speak and write wasn't on my life plan or agenda, and I didn't desire or crave the stage. I still don't. It isn't my first choice, but God has not called me to comfort, He has called me to work for the Kingdom in whatever capacity He chooses. My response is saying yes to submission and no to my selfish desires.

I am reminded of Esther's courage because her words could have cost her life. She, too, was called to speak, not before a crowd, but to a powerful king who held life and death in his hands. Her motive to press in wasn't out of selfishness but rather the desire to fulfill God's purpose - to save His chosen nation from genocide. God had put her in the right place at the right time.

I believe somewhere between verses 14 and 15 of chapter 4, Esther took courage. She did not take her courage but the courage of the Father. If she were to perish, at least she did what she knew was right. God gave her the courage even to face death.

Mordecai reminded her why this moment was important - God would save the people with or without her. You see, our obedience or disobedience will not change God's plan because we will be His instrument, or He will choose someone else, and we will miss the blessing. It is our choice to participate or not, but ultimately His plans will succeed with or without us.

God-given strength within us says, despite our cowardly ways, despite our fear in the outcome of saying yes to God, we trust You more than this. When God calls us to it, He gives us the desire for it. Does that make it easy? By no means. Does it make following God's call our best yes? Yes, it does.

I still have a fresh, holy fear before I step on a stage to speak. I pray that never goes away. It's my reminder to grab spiritual courage from the Father. The same girl who told God she would never speak now finds joy in the places that once felt impossible. It took being still in that hallway

Our weaknesses and deficiencies are where He will demonstrate His strength.

to let go of the fear that kept me bound and allow God to reveal the joy of walking in what He called me to do.

Spiritual courage doesn't make us great, it displays the power of Christ in us. Courage to do what God asks of us isn't found in ourselves but in Him. Our weaknesses and deficiencies are where He will demonstrate His strength. I think Paul's example describes it best in 2 Corinthians. A thorn in his flesh was given to keep him from exalting himself. His weakness kept him in a place of humility to see his desperate need of God for his weakest areas.

Knowing we cannot do it on our own is a gift because God's power is sufficient to use our weakness for the glory of the gospel.

"But he said to me, "My grace is sufficient for you, for my power is perfected in weakness." Therefore, I will boast all the more about my weaknesses, so that Christ's power may reside in me" (2 Corinthians 12:9).

CHAPTER NINE

The Mess of Prayer

Hannah (1 Samuel 1; 2:1-10)

I was like most little girls in that I had names picked out for all my baby dolls. I wrote their names in my notebooks and thought about what it would be like to be a mom one day. But that all changed the older I got and the more it seemed my life was not working out how I had planned.

I dreamed of a being a mom, all the while being a museum curator (I know, you probably just thought, I have never heard anyone say they dreamed about being a museum curator, but I did). I wanted to travel the world and see the art that I loved in books, but those dreams became a distant fantasy. The more destructive choices I made, the further I found myself from my dreams and even further from God.

I spent far too many years believing I had nothing of value to offer the world, much less tiny humans. I believed my choices disqualified me, my sins were too great, and my heart too broken for me to be anything more than a mess. That was until I met my Jesus.

For the first time in my life, I felt I had a future and in that future, I wanted a family.

Seeing that sentence makes it sound easy, but it was far from it. There was far more I felt God needed to do in the sanctification process of my life before He put a kid in my hands. There was healing I still needed before another life became my responsibility. And, just like the time I told God I would never speak in front of crowds, this was one of those moments where I am pretty sure God laughed at my plans.

(I feel like I can say this next part because we are friends now. We are in this, right? After all, if you made it to chapter nine, you're invested. So, since we are coffee-drinking-Bible-study-Jesus-loving friends, I'm going to lay out some hard truth.)

You know that foolish phrase people throw around (I used to do it, too), that God won't give you more than you can handle? This was the moment in my life when God proved that phrase was a crazy lie from the pit of hell.

Five months into our marriage the line on that little, white test stick was clearly turning into a plus sign. We wanted a family, but we had a different plan in mind about when that would happen. I had just turned twenty, we were still newlyweds, and now there would be a little person in the middle.

I was scared my entire pregnancy, wondering all the ways I might mess her up or do all the wrong things. Our precious daughter changed me in so many ways, but more than anything, she showed me how loved I am by God.

God used motherhood to teach me and unveil the truth of how He saw me. My love for my daughter was so indescribable. Every time I held her in my arms and rocked her in the rocking chair I was given a glimpse of how God cradles me in all things. When I held her tiny hand, I learned how God holds me up in the valleys of my life. Needless to say, being a mother changed my view of God.

This tiny human taught me God WILL give me more than I can handle, but He WILL be right there with me along the way.

Addison was barely two when I felt the longing in my heart to have another child. I began to pray and ask God every day for us to have another baby. We tried and struggled for over a year. I never stopped asking. Some of those prayers were knitted together with my tears. I hate to admit my selfishness, but I was discontent with just one child in my arms. I failed to see my selfish heart was pushing me from God rather than to Him. My prayers were hollow, vain words I cast into the air as if I was asking a genie for a magic wish.

God is not a magic wish machine, no matter how good or beautiful the things are we ask for. His plans are perfect and not without purpose.

I prayed for a year and asked God for a second child; it was the greatest desire of my heart. When we finally received a positive pregnancy test, I just knew God had answered my prayers. I knew He had given me the desire of my heart, but I didn't realize this would be the season when God would teach me that He doesn't always answer our prayers as we hope, and there would be things I could not handle in my own strength.

I sat in the doctor's office excited and impatient to check up on our new little peanut growing in my belly. My three-year-old daughter was pacing the floor sharing all that was happening in her little mind. I had prayed so fervently for this new life, we were ready to grow our family.

The doctor waved the heart monitor over my twelve-week belly and found nothing.

He couldn't find a heartbeat.

We picked up the crayons and coloring books and were ushered into the ultrasound room to check up on our sweet baby only to find a precious small body, but no beating heart.

The tears were instant and uncontrollable. All the chatter from my daughter came to a stop. The world skidded to a halt.

But, I had prayed...I asked God for a baby, and He blessed us. He gave us this child, so why would He take it away? What had I done wrong? How was I going to tell my husband? Our family and friends? I did not prepare for this; miscarriage wasn't supposed to happen.

In the hard places, in the deepest valleys, in the darkest of nights is where God comes the most real to us.

Maybe devastated isn't the right word to use for what I felt. I felt like I had failed to keep safe what God had given. In the previous three years we had welcomed our daughter, buried my Father, and had already experienced one miscarriage. Now... another one. I was ravaged and undone. My heart burned within my chest and I wondered if I was being punished for all the terrible choices I had made in my life.

The words, "Your baby isn't alive," put me a million light-years away from God.

I remember the phrase, "God won't give you more than you can handle; you are strong." No, I was not strong. I was hurt and I felt more alone than ever. I wanted God to answer my prayers my way. I didn't like His way.

He was the God of my salvation, but now, He was becoming a God who took away everything I wanted. My deepest fears seemed to be unraveling within His hands. How could a God who loved me allow so much pain?

In the hard places, in the deepest valleys, in the darkest of nights is where God becomes the most real to us. Not because we are sufficient in ourselves, but because in the aches of our heart we see our genuine need for God.

Drunken Prayer

The journey to worship at the temple was a time Hannah dreaded, but also took solace in. She knew what it meant. Elkanah, her husband, loved and treasured her, and maybe even took pity on her because she could not bear him children as she hoped. He wanted to be enough for her, but her heart's desire was to do what the culture told her was her only job, bear children.

She was taunted by more than a barren womb. She was tormented by her sister-wife, Peninnah, and her fruitful womb.

This journey was different than all the other times. It was as if Hannah was even more aware of her failures and the undeniable desires of her heart. I imagine she felt forgotten by God, the God who gives life. She agonized over the round bellies she saw pass her by, and I am sure she wondered, "Why not me? Why has God forgotten me?"

She fell hard to her knees on the stone ground of the temple. The unbearable weight of grief ripped through her empty womb, and echoed louder with every beat beneath her chest. Her desire was nothing more than to be a mother, to carry a child and be remembered by God. The ache of her heart was so loud it bellowed even to the ears of passers-by.

Her sobs were so violent no sound could come from her mouth and her body shook under the agony that held her heart captive. It didn't matter who was standing by watching. It was her time alone with

God in her bubble of sorrow. Her lips moved quickly though not a noise was made between the tears.

Her real need wasn't for a child: her Truest need was God alone.

Hannah had high hopes for a family when she married. She never dreamed she would be a barren woman. This moment on the stone floor of the synagogue, she pleaded with God. Being deeply hurt made her desperately move toward the Father. She moved into a posture of petition to the only One who could give her the greatest desire of her heart - a child.

I can hear her promise to God woven through her prayers, this child, she would give back to Him. All the days of his life would be sanctified to God alone. She gripped her chest over her heart as she breathed out, "Remember me" (1 Samuel 1:11).

Hannah had to come to a place of utter surrender to receive the peace she needed.

Eli, the high priest, was confident this woman was drunk, and when he approached her with a voice of accusation, Hannah didn't waver, "No, my Lord," Hannah replied. "I am a woman with a broken heart. I haven't had any wine or beer; I've been pouring out my heart before the Lord. Don't think of me as a wicked woman; I've been praying from the depth of my anguish and resentment" (1 Samuel 15-16, CSB). Her passion was not for her plight, but for the Father. She knew this circumstance was beyond anything she could control in her own power.

When Hannah rose up from her prayers, "her face was no longer sad" (1 Samuel 1:18).

She had no way of knowing if she would indeed bear a child as she had asked God for, but she had faith to rise up from her knees and trust that God was greater. He showered her with His peace and she was confident in Him.

Her real need wasn't for a child; her truest need was God alone.

God heard the prayers of Hannah and remembered her. He opened her womb and gave her a son, a son that would be entirely devoted to the Lord.

Hannah knew the only Source she needed was God, for He held the answers she craved. She laid her burden out and left it in His hands. When she arose, she was no longer sad. Hannah had faith God would meet her in her trouble, even if it didn't turn out as she had hoped.

Rise Up

After our second miscarriage, the devastation ravaged me.

I didn't pray anymore; I didn't know how.

I didn't talk about it; I had nothing to say.

I was plagued with grief and questions. I was confused about the outcome of the prayer I so fervently begged God to give me.

The grief was heavy after our loss, and it became a profoundly broken and weak season in my life. But, looking back I am reminded God answered my prayer according to His plan.

Now, I look to the future with hope to see our child's face for the first time one day when I reach heaven.

I look at my present to our sweet middle son who would not be here if God had not answered my prayers according to His perfect will. In that, God allows me soft glimpses that He has a bigger plan in place.

God knows what we need before we need it because He knows the plan before it happens.

I look to the past and see how God used those moments to pull and stretch my faith and teach me to trust in Him for not only my salvation, but for my everyday need of the gospel.

Losing a child leaves unimaginable emptiness and crippling pain. We pray, we plead, and we beg for God to give us our greatest desires, to give us what we think is best, rather than what He has prepared for us. We fervently pray and seek the Father with every fiber of who we are. We pour out our heart's desires, our deepest longings, and greatest need.

His answer to our prayer may not be the picture we want painted. You see, God knows what we need before we need it because He knows the plan before it happens.

"For my thoughts are not your thoughts, neither are your ways my ways, declares the Lord" (Isaiah 55:8).

We send up prayers to heaven in hopes God will hear our cries, but most often our prayers are bathed in our desires and come only in our times of need. I have filled prayer journals with my own needs and very little praise to the One who answers those prayers. Prayers go up, and we expect God to send only blessings down.

All that time I wrestled with God because I leaned on myself. That was until I learned that leaning on myself gave me nothing to stand on. I needed the lessons my Heavenly Father taught me as I held my daughter - how He would cradle me in all things and hold me up in the valleys of life.

God isn't just the God of salvation. He isn't a God who simply gives us what we want and desire. He is omniscient (all-knowing), omnipresent (everywhere), sovereign (knows all and controls all), merciful, and gracious.

When Hannah brought Samuel to the temple, she offered a prayer we can learn whole-heartedly from:

"There is none holy like the Lord:

For there is none besides you;

There is no rock like our God.

Talk no more so very proudly,

Let not arrogance come from your mouth;

For the Lord is a God of knowledge,

and by him actions are weighed" (2 Samuel 2:2-3).

Hannah learned something we too learn as God answers our prayers according to His will; we cannot let our arrogance and selfishness come before a holy God.

Without prayer we are powerless because it fortifies our faith, our armor. It is the very key to unlocking the resurrection power within us. Each part of becoming more like Jesus and being sanctified by the Spirit requires prayer.

Prayer is often the piece of my walk with Jesus I struggle with the most. Never having been truly discipled and taught about prayer, I could only imitate what I heard others pray. However, it never felt like it was my own, even forced to fit my mouth at times. The craving as a child of God for authentic prayer wraps around our bones and won't let go. It is the Spirit calling out from within us to the Father.

Our most passionate prayers should not be reserved just for the deepest valleys of our lives; they should be our everyday conversations with our Abba Father. We need to begin speaking to God and allow the Spirit of God to teach us how to pray.

Our prayers don't have to be perfect. Prayer more often than not feels messy. It can be written in a journal, on your knees, in a prayer room, with hands folded or open. Our prayers are heartfelt cries to the One who knows us better than we know ourselves.

Prayer is how we lean in when God gives us more than we can handle.

"Hear my prayer, O Lord; give ear to my pleas for mercy! In your faithfulness answer me, in your righteousness!" (Psalm 143:1).

"Rejoice in hope, be patient in tribulation, be constant in prayer" (Romans 12:12).

Pray When It's Hard

I trust God more than my pain.

There are precious women in my life who never saw a happy ending to their prayers for children. There is still a soft sting within their flesh because every answer we long for may not be the answer we get. For some reason, by which only God knows, it may be what we need. As much as that sentence pains my heart, and it is hard for me to wrap my humanity-limited brain around, I trust God more than my pain.

In the hardest times when it seems the most difficult to pray or the most difficult seasons to understand, God is shaping us, molding us into His greatest masterpiece. The answers or lack of answers to our prayer end up being what we need to make us more like Him, to teach us to lean a bit harder on YAHWEH our God.

Hannah shows us her prayer of anguish in 1 Samuel 1:10. Her prayer was so emotional she was mistaken for a drunk, but there is no mistaking the prayers of the heartbroken. We can pray prayers of pain, but what about the prayers of our Mondays, the mundane prayers of our every days. The pleading for health, breath, wisdom, and direction. The whispers for peace and yes, even patience.

Prayer is our most vulnerable position with the Father.

Hannah isn't the only one who teaches us prayer is messy; we cannot read a Psalm of David without seeing there is nothing neat and tidy about prayer. It is the best and worst of who we are exiting our mouths in petition, praise, promise, and power. Our words have no need of being manicured, edited, or even spelled correctly. But here is what they should be, exactly how we feel, not sugar-coated, but just downright real.

Prayer is our most vulnerable position with the Father.

He is our Yahweh, Abba, Alpha, and Omega. He is the great I AM, Creator, Master, Redeemer, and our greatest Friend.

With our best friends we spare no details when we spill our deepest fears and greatest joys out onto the table. That is what our daily prayers should be. God already knows our needs and desires, but He longs for our communication with Him. He wants us to bring it to Him before we take it anywhere else.

The worn knee prints next to the bed, the tears shed in the carpool line, and the journals filled with coffee stains, those are the places He will meet us. Every single morning, in every single prayer, when our hearts are repentant, and our words simple. He will meet us in the hospital rooms, in the doctor's office with test results, even as we hold the hand of the dying; God will meet us in prayer. He will bend His ear to our needs, and He will bring comfort when we need it.

The God of all comfort knew what was taking place in my life, and my heart knows it was allowed for a purpose. God may not always answer our prayers our way, and sometimes, His answer to our prayer may break our hearts. But, He is faithful to provide what we need in our circumstance.

"Blessed be the God and Father of our Lord Jesus Christ, the Father of mercies and God of all comfort, who comforts us in all our affliction, so that we may be able to comfort those who are in an affliction, with the comfort with which we ourselves are comforted by God" (2 Corinthians 1:2-4).

Hannah knew the One who held life in His hands, the One who could make a way for her to have a child, and the One who would offer comfort if it wasn't His plan. We, too, know the One who holds all things within His hands, even when the answer is no, or even when it remains unanswered.

"Continue steadfastly in prayer, being watchful in it with thanksgiving" (Colossians 4:2).

CHAPTER TEN
The Mess of Obedience
Deborah (Judges 4-5)

It's a rainy Monday. The noise level inside my house is through the roof. My coffee is cold because I have spent more time commanding obedience from the little people in my care than I have to drink it. I have asked for the tenth time in an hour for a chore to be completed or math work to be done. It's on days like these I am ready to crawl back into my bed and pull the covers over my head and wave my white flag of surrender.

Now don't get me wrong, I have pretty awesome kids, if I do say so myself. They are hooligans, but they get that from their dad, so it's ok. They have bad days, and lose their minds most days ending in Y, but we recover, and all is well before bedtime (somedays). Then again, I am the same way.

I start out really well. I get up early, read my Bible, and pray. But, by lunch time I want to curl up in the fetal position and beg for mercy. By the time the day ends, my time in the Word is a distant memory, and my prayers feel empty. Then I get up the next day and do it all again.

Have I mentioned being a mom is hard, sanctifying work requiring spiritual courage and all that?

I learned something recently that changed everything and brought me out of mom-survival-mode and into the light. I realized I needed to rely on God as more than my morning fill up. I had to learn that I needed God in my life - every minute, second, and millisecond of the day.

You see, when I closed His Word and said amen, I left God there. I didn't take Him with me when I left my Bible study spot. I kept God limited to my early morning Bible reading and prayer journals.

I boxed God in.

The mess of obedience is found in the surrender.

When we put God in a box we make Him nothing more than a one-time God, and when we put limitations on Him, we are unable to see His power.

I put God there, and because He was just a "God of the morning" in my life, it was easy to say no to Him for all the other things. I wasn't walking in obedience.

We are all tilted toward disobedience.

There is a connection here between obedience and survival – just as there is a connection to mess and surrender. Where these two things converge, we find rest in Christ.

Obedience is monumental in our Christian walk; it is the act of submitting to God's authority and then living it out - by choice. The mess of obedience is found in the surrender. If we don't surrender our will to God, then disobedience will have its way.

We have tackled all these messes – the ones we make, the ones we cannot control, and now the messes that come in being His daughter. Each one is difficult to walk out but they are messes we willingly allow God to make in us. Over and over again. Why?

Because choosing Jesus is better.

Here is what I know - I cannot be obedient as long as my selfish pride is in the way. God won't put up with my folded arms and nose in the air, resisting all He has for me. He won't idly wait around while I continue to repeatedly say no.

Choosing Jesus will always be better.

The mess of obedience means forging a way that will feel like it goes directly against the grain of our sinful flesh because obedience is all part of us becoming more like Jesus.

The transformation of salvation leads to obedience, obedience is key to sanctification, and sanctification gives way to devotion. The life being sanctified is a process with the ultimate end of glorification. (Basically, God is making us more like Jesus every day, which will ultimately end in Heaven.)

This process isn't for us, sure there are benefits and blessings, but the object is to glorify God above all else.

"For those who he foreknew he also predestined to be conformed to the image of his Son, in order that he might be the firstborn among many brothers" (Romans 8:29).

The prince of preachers, Charles Spurgeon, puts obedience like this, "Do what the Lord bids you, where he bids you, as he bids you, as long as he bids you, and do it at once."[5] Yes, obedience requires full action, not always without question, but without hesitation. I haven't always taken the first step of obedience well, and sometimes I still don't.

The transformation from salvation leads to obedience. obedience is the key to sanctification. and sanctification gives way to devotion.

Sometimes I even feel the nudge of the Spirit to do something, and I blatantly say no, because it feels easier to say, "I don't want to" than to do the hard things.

Our disobedience is a flat out no in the face of God. Choosing not to listen is saying our way is better, or more comfortable than what God is asking of us. It can feel easier to pick what makes us happy rather than what makes us holy.

Obedience is choosing to follow God's lead even when we are acting like my kids; kicking and screaming our way to do what is asked of us. I look at my children, and I see myself. I see the struggles I have in obeying my Heavenly Father.

Do you remember a few chapters back when I shared a story with you about a transition our family had in ministry? Well, now seems like a great time to finish the story.

We spent a season waiting for answers and a clearer picture of what God was asking of us. God eventually made it clear, and what He was asking seemed far bigger than the ability we had within ourselves. Not to mention it would be far bigger than our comfort would allow. But, here is the thing about following God – if He has a direction for you to go, He will make it very clear that it is His call.

Everything we encountered in those many months pointed us back to one thing – obedience. Every sermon, conversation, school lesson, and Bible study centered on the same thing – obedience. There was no denying what God was saying. My husband and I became clear on one thing. We owed God our yes.

Our freedom is what fuels us with the desire for obedience.

"So if the Son sets you free, you will be free indeed" (John 8:36).

"For freedom Christ has set us free; stand firm therefore, and do not submit again to a yoke of slavery" (Galatians 5:1).

God revealed so much of the Gospel to us in every step we took. Our power or works do not save us. Therefore, we are not saved by our strength or our actions. We are redeemed for God's divine plans and purposes alone.

We see obedience in Scripture, and we also see endless disobedience. Abraham obeyed God when commanded to sacrifice his son Isaac, and a ram was provided in his place. Paul obeyed God after his conversion and brought people to repentance. Moses obeyed God and crossed the Red Sea. Jonah disobeyed God when he was told to go to Ninevah and found himself in the belly of a BIG fish. The Israelites throughout the Old Testament continually disobeyed, but we see God continued to offer solutions for His children, one of which came in the form of a willing judge named Deborah.

Under the Palm of Deborah

The Israelites were known for their continual disobedience. From their rescue out of Egypt and their time in wilderness, to wars with rivals and waiting for the Promised Land, God's people would fall into the same pattern - obey for a little while, then turn away from God. Their history was predictable; they found themselves in the same place time and again. God's solution was to establish judges in Israel. The judges would lead the people and preside over them and attempt to keep them out of trouble. Deborah was the fifth judge to lead the people of God, and the only woman to do so.

Each judge was raised by God Himself to lead and deliver His people. In a time when women didn't play a leading role, God raised up Deborah to help deliver His people Israel. Now we can't go on with Deborah's story until we see this next part.

"And the people of Israel AGAIN did what was evil in the sight of the Lord after Ehud died" (Judges 4:1, emphasis mine).

Seriously? Again? But, then again, I am no different.

They came to her by the dozens as she sat under the shade of the tree. They knew just where to find her even in the heat of the day, and she would pass judgement on the people.

I'd like to think Deborah had incredible confidence in God, not because she was a judge, but because she trusted Him for all things.

She, like the judges before her, could push the Israelites toward obedience. The judges served as a makeshift savior for the people (not a permanent solution but a temporary fix). There was a pattern with God's people; they disobeyed God and made Him angry, He delivered them to their enemies, they cried out for help, and God would send a judge to their rescue.

Does this sound familiar?

God's chosen people disobeyed Him by way of sin.

They lived with the consequences of sin.

They cried out to God for a Messiah.

God sends Jesus.

Jesus rescues them from sin.

~

* **We were born into sin, "there is none righteous no not one" (Romans 3:23).**

  - We are born into a life separated from God through sin. We have no way to God without a Savior; what we earn from sin is death (eternal separation from God).

* **"For the wages of sin is death, but the gift of God is eternal life through Jesus Christ our Lord" (Romans 6:28).**

  - Jesus, the perfect Son of God, was sent to pay the penalty for our sins for all time.

* **"But God demonstrates His own love toward us, in that while we were still sinners, Christ died for us" (Romans 5:8).**

  - Jews and Gentiles alike can receive the gift of salvation.

* **"For I am not ashamed of the gospel, for it is the power of God for salvation to everyone who believes, to the Jew first and also to the Greek" (Romans 1:16).**

  - We no longer bear the punishment ourselves.

* **"Since, therefore, we have now been justified by his blood, much more shall we be saved by him from the wrath of God" (Romans 5:9).**

~

Since Jesus' time hadn't yet come, the judges had their place in leading Israel.

Deborah sought to rouse them out of their comfortable places of disobedience - her determination, set by God, was to see His people finally free; their captivity removed once and for all. God revealed His plan to her of how they would win the battle against the Cananities. She needed an army leader and chose Barak to do the job. He would lead

121

God's people to victory. But, Barak, being a smart guy, knew they didn't stand a chance without her giving the commands.

Despite the terrible consistency of God's people, despite knowing they would probably rebel against God and fall into the same pattern again and again, Deborah chose to be faithful to God. Because, unlike His people, God was faithful to His word.

They didn't have just any enemy they were up against. Canaan was the promised land, but the people who inhabited it were far from God's promised people. They worshipped many gods and prided themselves on the sexualized aspect of their religion, complete with temple prostitutes.

Sisera, the leader of the army of Canaan, had been vicious toward the Israelites for many years, and it was time to put an end to his reign of terror. Sisera commanded an army of 100,000 men and had 900 iron chariots, each one stronger than the last. When Deborah called the Israelites to battle only 10,000 followed behind Barak. Their numbers were weak, but the will of their God was their strength.

God threw the Canaanites into confusion and sent them fleeing, including Sisera. It didn't slow the Israelites' pursuit. Sisera sought refuge in the tent of Jael, believing she would be his rescue. Jael would have known he was fleeing battle and that the Israelites would soon be behind him.

In God's narrative, you are entirely at His mercy; the enemies of Israel could not and would not stand. Jael comforted Sisera, lulled him into a false sense of peace and drove a tent stake through his temple and into the ground. (Seriously, and to think people find the Old Testament boring!)

"And behold, as Barak was pursuing Sisera, Jael went out to meet him and said to him, "Come, and I will show you the man whom you are seeking." So he went in to her tent, and there lay Sisera dead, with the tent peg in his temple" (Judges 4:22). Bringing Sisera down was the key to subduing the king.

The Israelites grew in strength under the leadership of Deborah until the king of Canaan was destroyed. This victory by the hands of God alone, left the people with a land that could rest at last from the wars that ravaged them and the bondage that chased them. Forty years of peace, at last, fell upon the people of Israel.
(Until they disobeyed again, but that's for another chapter in a different book.)

Obey All the Way

We could share a lot of coffee over this topic, settling in and talking about what obedience looks like in your life and mine. We could wrestle through our pride that keeps us from moving forward, and kick back fears that bind us up in our comfort zones. But, if there is anything I could say to you right now it would be that saying yes to God is always worth it.

Saying yes to God is always worth it.

My family's call to ministry and Deborah's story are examples of life-altering steps of obedience. But, what about the small steps?

What about the everyday "yeses" to God?

Yes, to fighting for your marriage.

Yes, to raising tiny humans.

Yes, to ministering to those around you.

Yes, to offering help to someone who needs it.

Yes, to opening your Bible and being with God daily.

Deborah chose obedience when the people around her were notorious for their lack of it. Generations of history displayed the on again, off again relationship Israel had with God. Deborah was no stranger to her people's actions or, better yet, inaction. This woman, considered to be a prophetess and a judge of the people, had likely grown tired of their lack of faith. I know I probably would have.

This need for obedience is wrapped up in our need for Jesus and is perfectly described in Romans 5:19, "For as by the one man's disobedience (Adam) the many were made sinners, so by the one man's obedience (Jesus) the many will be made righteous" (emphasis mine). Without the obedience of Jesus we are lost and without hope, all of these words would have been for nothing, and there would be no holy to meet us right here in our mess.

Obedience is what drives faith forward, and our willingness to be carriers of the gospel is because Christ was obedient to the cross. Romans continues with the reminder about the power of obedience in chapter 6 verse 16, "Don't you know that if you offer yourselves to someone as obedient slaves, you are slaves of that one you obey - either of sin leading to death or of obedience leading to righteousness?"

Being obedient to God often asks us to step into an uncomfortable place. The choice then becomes will we be obedient and uncomfortable, or disobedient and comfortable (temporarily). The more nos we give to God, the less likely I think He will be to ask again. If we are believers, obedience is always the right answer.

Friend, be reminded, we choose who we will obey.

God, or the world.

Sin and death, or Jesus and the resurrected life.

Deborah also reminds us that often obedience is required if we are to be warriors of the faith. This woman who fought for God's people, whose words and actions consistently pointed to God was called "The mother of Israel." Can we say the same for ourselves? As friends, wives, mamas, sisters, and daughters does our reputation cry out obedience to Christ? Do we let Jesus affect every role in our lives?

We see obedience in her song of victory in Judges 5. Deborah was faithful, but fully gave credit where it was due, to the Lord alone. "Hear, O kings, give ear, O princes; to the Lord I will sing; I will make melody to the Lord, the God of Israel" (Judges 5:3).

A Swahili Proverb speaks of who we are as warriors and holy daughters; let this settle on your heart, "The daughter of a lion is also a lion." Within us is the power of the Lion, our God who is the Lion of Judah. We are His daughters and wholly belong to Him alone. He is who we seek to obey and with our obedience we become warriors of faith, just as Deborah was.

Within us is the power of the Lion, our God who is the Lion of Judah.

"Jesus answered, "If anyone [really] loves Me, he will keep My word (teaching); and My Father will love him, and WE will come to him and make Our dwelling place with him. One who does not [really] love Me does not keep My words. And the word (teaching) which you hear is not Mine, but is the Father's who sent Me" (John 14:23-24, AMP).

CHAPTER ELEVEN
The Mess of Transformation
Rahab (Joshua 2-6)

There was a time in my life when I didn't understand people who loved Jesus. I mean really loved Him. I pretended to get it though because that is what people do, right? I wore my W.W.J.D. bracelet and went to church camp on occasion, but I didn't get it. Nothing about it seemed so important that it should matter in my life more than anything else. I mean I went to church now and then when my mom told me to. I went to youth group because I had a crush on the cute boy, but that's pretty standard for most teenage girls.

That was good enough, right?

We live in a culture that has taught us for generations that just being "good" is enough.

I walked down the aisle at church, knelt at an altar and they sprinkled my head and gave me a necklace. I couldn't earn those things until after I took a class where I vividly remember them asking me to draw a picture of what I thought Jesus looked like.

That was good enough, right?

Enough for God to like me?

Enough for me to feel ok with my standing in God's eyes?

Enough for me to continue sinning without worrying, right?

The older I got, true brokenness and new sins entered the picture, but I wasn't concerned. After all, no one else in my life was. I wasn't overwhelmed with conviction. I was a teenager, drugs and alcohol were normal, so they became my crutch. Meaningless relationships were permitted and accepted, so they became my attempt at mending my brokeness. All while still wearing my W.W.J.D. bracelet.

This is what it meant to be good enough?

For many years Jesus was simply what I drew on a piece of paper in a confirmation class. He wasn't personal or real in my life. The illusion of being enough was a distorted trap keeping me just out of reach of the gospel, similar to keeping a homeless person's food and shelter just out of sight but only a few feet away.

I was ruined and blind to sin, lied to, and tricked into believing I was ok as long as I did what everyone else did. Over time the reality of sin began to rip away at my insides, destroying me, slowly, piece by piece, until I no longer recognized the girl that stared back at me. I took off and threw away my W.W.J.D bracelet. To that girl, Jesus didn't matter. I realized the bracelet didn't and couldn't change me; neither could the necklace around my neck and the sprinkled water on my head.

The enemy taunted me with the memories of every mistake and misstep I had ever taken. He had won. Or so he thought. Little by little I remembered this Jesus I had been told about in my grandparents' Sunday school class when I was small, listening to conversations in passing, songs that played on the radio in my youth leader's car, and the Bible my mother gave me.

None of those things could eternally save my soul, but God used each piece to woo my broken heart. It was as if specks of light began to break through my horrible darkness. I look back now and see the war that was raging for my soul. Thankfully, God wasn't leaving without me.

I had to be brought to a place where I saw I was not enough apart from Christ. All of those years believing just a head knowledge of God and a picture drawn with crayons in a class at church wasn't enough to secure me to salvation. I trusted in the false hope that we can do enough to get to heaven.

"He has delivered us from the domain of darkness and transferred us to the kingdom of his beloved Son, in whom we have redemption, the forgiveness of sins" (Colossians 1:13-14).

The mess of transformation comes when God changes who we used to be into who He longs for us to become. Transformation cannot happen without salvation, which is the catalyst that begins a lifelong process of sanctification. Being sanctified is a process by which we become more like Christ (holy) as our lives are used according to His purpose and plan. It involves the testing of our faith and the trying of our flesh.

Being sanctified reminds me a lot of the TV show Fixer Upper (except it cannot be done in an hour). God chooses us in our rough and broken state. He knows the potential lying behind those broken floorboards of selfishness, our unstable foundation of pride, and the terrible wallpaper of vanity. And God is ready for demo day, except

The mess of Transformation comes when God changes who we used to be into who He longs for us to become.

the demolition process is lifelong. He corrects the foundation first through salvation and then begins to lay new floors of holiness and peel off the ugly wallpaper coated in our sins and hurts. He breathes fresh life into what had long been discarded, and just like Fixer Upper, He gives a new name. Yes! This is being sanctified and the result is beautiful and perfect. When we stand before God at the end of our lives, with the sanctification process complete, the reveal will be before the Lord.

The process is long and hard, and there will be bumps in the road as God changes us from the inside out. But, that is the beauty of transformation, it is God alone that sees our fullest potential and He alone knows what we will become.

To others we may look like a disaster, but to God we are infinitely beautiful!

More Than a Prostitute

Rahab's life within the city walls of Jericho was one of prostitution. How she got there isn't made clear to us, but what is, is her desire to leave it all behind. There is something about her I deeply identify with, maybe it was her desire for more than the terrible life she found herself living.

Anyone content in their bad situation won't jump at the chance of rescue.

The God of Israel would have been the topic of tales from the time Rahab was a child - from His parting of the Red Sea to the daily manna He provided to His mysterious cloud by day and pillar of fire by night. In her estimation, the God of Israel was unlike the gods worshipped in Jericho.

There is much I could speculate about how this story went down. I can just imagine the courage and faith it took for her to hide the spies, walls crashing down around her, and then waiting for rescue. There was no doubt however that faith, a saving faith, changed this woman. This faith kept her from the rubble and destruction others in Jericho faced.

True transformation requires saving faith.

One thing I love about God is He uses the unlikely, the discarded, and the overlooked. He uses the ones you would least expect by the world's standards. Thank goodness for that.

True Transformation requires saving faith.

"God has chosen what is insignificant and despised in the world - what is viewed as nothing - to bring to nothing what is viewed as something so that no one may boast in his presence" (1 Corinthians 1:28-29).

Jericho heard rumors of the Israelites' approach, but also knew the Jordan River stood between them. The fortified city with thick, imposing walls was probably lulled into a false sense of security, but I have a feeling Rahab knew something else bigger was about to take place. From her perch she saw the spies come into the city; she knew they were different and took a leap of faith.

Rahab began to tell the men all she knew of God, and how God had given them the land of Jericho to conquer. She recounted the acts of God that had been so astounding, and she pleaded that they would spare her life. Rahab declared, "The Lord your God, he is God in the heavens above and the earth beneath" (Joshua 2:11).

Rahab had faith God would spare her life and the lives of her family. She threw a long scarlet rope out of her window and let the men climb down the wall of the city to safety. She believed in her heart freedom would come. To her, it must have felt simple, while her family thought it to be an impossible faith.

The spies left one instruction with her, hang the scarlet cord from the window to identify her house as the home of the woman who had helped them in their time of need. She and her family would be spared from destruction only if they were inside her house.

God was changing Rahab, changing her from the woman she was into the woman He wanted her to be.

Charles Spurgeon says this of Rahab's faith, "This woman's faith was saving faith, singular faith, stable faith, self-denying faith, sympathizing faith, and sanctifying faith."[6]

She watched and listened for seven days as the Israelites marched in silence around the walls of the city. What were they doing? Why did they not attack? On the seventh day she sat at her window and heard a sudden break in the silence, the blast of trumpets and the shout of thousands. The house began to shake like a great earthquake as she saw the walls of the city crumble before her eyes.

The Israelites rushed the city. The spies opened the door of Rahab's home, grabbed her family and ran. There was blood on the ground under her feet and deafening screams among the rubble. The destruction of this city symbolized the destruction of who she used to be.

The thing about transformation is we cannot continue to carry the burden and weight of our past sin. God whispers, "Give them to me. Let me bear their weight."

The spies took her and her family to the camp of the Israelites as they watched Jericho go up in flames. Israel was now her people, and their God became her God. Rahab looked back at the city, this place she had called home and found it destroyed, laid waste by the weight of its evil and sin. But, she was safe. Her faith had saved her.

Change Me

I trusted God for salvation and believed Him for my future and hope. But, I struggled to trust God to entirely remove my past. How could God thoroughly wash away all the terrible things I had done in my life? It took years of building what I call "faith muscles" (the only kind of somewhat toned muscles I have in my body). God had discarded my past the day I surrendered it all to Him. But, my mind hadn't.

The enemy enjoys harassing me with my terrible choices, trying to convince me my salvation was all a trick, and that God would never forgive a girl like me. I am vulnerable to my past, and the enemy knows it. Even now almost 14 years later, my history still comes to mind occasionally, usually when the enemy wants to discredit me or cut me at the knees.

Not today Satan, not today.

I wrote a letter to God a few weeks after I gave my life to Christ. A letter detailing every single thing I could remember doing, on paper it looked like the worst of the worst. It was tear stained and worn from rubbing it with my hands. I wonder if Rahab looked at her life like I did and thought, "How did it get this bad? This out of control? How could God forgive me for this much?"

I found the list a few years back and cried heavily over the page in my hand. That girl seems like a distant and faded memory because

Transformation by the hands of the Father is messy as He molds us into His holy daughters.

God did so much to change me. It has been messy, this process of transforming me into the person God desires for me to be.

God is making a mess of me in the best possible way, every single day. I pray He never stops. With every word I write, and with every group of women I teach, I pray He makes a mess of me from now until I stand in His presence.

Transformation by the hands of the Father is messy as He molds us into His holy daughters.

Have you heard the saying, "Sometimes you have to make a bigger mess before you can really clean it up?" That's the motto of my spring cleaning, or the desire to organize that comes with book writing (it's called organizational procrastination; I named it, so it's a thing). My closets, drawers, and cabinets are never cleaner than when I have a deadline. But, it never fails, I have to make a bigger mess for progress to happen - throwing out the old things, sorting the good things into organized bins, or putting stuff in storage. There are usually trash bags everywhere and mountains of stuff needing to be donated.

As God works out the old in us, as He changes us, it doesn't always come easy. Being sanctified comes with struggle and even a little bit of pain. There are things that need to be bagged up and thrown out. But, it is needed for His glory and the results are for our benefit.

Rahab wouldn't be who we would have chosen to fulfill God's purpose, but I am not who you would have wanted either. Every woman or man chosen by God is imperfect and flawed, but with Him all things are possible. Every person has potential in Christ because they are transformed with purpose and changed by His incredible power.

Rahab's story didn't end there in Jericho or with her escape from destruction. She married a man who would equip her in continuing the line that would lead to Christ, a line that would bring about a man named Boaz, who would marry a beautiful woman named Ruth. Their lineage would lead to Obed, then Jesse, then David and ultimately, Jesus. A lineage of sinners reminds us it is in Christ we are forgiven and redeemed, and who God uses is of His choosing.

We cannot bring the holy; the only things that rest in our hands are the messes we have made. I want nothing more than to be transformed by God through His Holy Spirit, by the blood of Jesus Christ on a cross, and by His Word as I read it every day.

Faith Fuel

The book of Joshua isn't the last place we are reminded of the faith of Rahab. "By faith Rahab the prostitute was not destroyed along with those who were disobedient, because she had welcomed the spies [sent by the sons of Israel] in peace" (Hebrews 11:31). Our faith plays a part in our transformation. Faith that God is better, faith strong enough to surrender it all at His feet.

A life of sin will keep us bound and trapped by the walls built around us, but a life in Christ frees us and tears down every wall to get to our hearts. This new life brings with it healing, forgiveness, and grace upon amazing grace.

In Galatians 2:20 Paul reminds us, "I have been crucified with Christ. It is no longer I who live, but Christ who lives in me. And the life I now live in the flesh I live by faith in the Son of God, who loved me and gave himself for me." Our sin died with Christ upon the cross. We now live by faith because of what Jesus did in giving Himself for us.

Our transformation means we are not who we used to be, we are raised to a new life in Christ. Rahab received a new life and the same is available for us too. This transformation isn't out of reach; it is quite simply one call away. Give God room to be God, give Him the space to transform your life.

CHAPTER TWELVE

The Mess of Devotion

Mary Magdalene (John 19-20)

My sweet Granny's hands were frail, her skin pale and worn with time. Her eyes were full of patience, and her hair was white with years of wisdom. The heart within her chest beat with the rhythm of salvation, and the blood in her veins pumped with the sound of grace. She carried our family's faith legacy beautifully at the age of ninety-two.

When I looked at her aged hands, I saw every meal she cooked for us, the many blankets crocheted, and hugs given. They tell of her devoted years as a mom of three, grandmother of seven, and great-grandmother of ten; each one loved with great joy. Her hands had always been cold, and she lived out the adage, *Cold hands mean a warm heart.* She recently reminded me, however, she didn't always have a warm heart; sometimes it was loving, and other times it was correcting. She told me God gives us the exact heart we need, and He gave her one for her family.

She would be the first to tell you she had experienced a life full of God's grace and goodness. Like the rest of us, I saw in her eyes the hurts that had settled in over the years, the losses she faced when burying her husband, oldest daughter, and sisters. Then there were the hurts I am sure she never shared, the hardships of life swept under the rug. Nevertheless, every moment, good or bad, shaped her into the incredibly strong woman she was.

Granny never wavered in her faith, and just like the Proverbs 31 woman, strength and honor were her clothing. Her life was devoted fully to Jesus. In her early months of sickness after her heart attack, I would read the worn pages of her Bible to her when she could no longer hold it in her hands. I sat on the edge of her bed and read Psalm 23 and watched her aged mouth move with the words of Scripture that gave her hope. The God of the universe had faithfully sustained her, and it is a beautiful reminder that He will sustain me, too.

We think a life of devotion to Jesus is supposed to be extravagant with significant successes to our name. Sometimes we imagine an obedient and fruitful life of service to God looks like packed churches, altars filled, and wonderfully written Bible studies and books. To God, I think it looks like the hands of my grandmother. Worn, not from extravagant actions, but from devotion to the ones God gave her to shepherd and love. Those were the precious hearts He placed within her home to share Jesus with by simply being the woman He made her to be.

For her, devotion to the Father looked like changing diapers, cooking meals, and cleaning toilets. It looked like faithfully loving her husband through fifty-seven years of marriage. Faithfulness looked like diligently teaching Sunday school each week to children who needed to hear the gospel. It was serving wholeheartedly without recognition or acknowledgment.

Being devoted to Christ is a life wholly given to God, rooted in love, desire, and beautiful healing.

Whole and Healed

Mary Magdalene was chained in bondage with her mind warped and worn from constant invasion. Her tormented soul was continually plagued by demons who held her captive against her will; she was mentally unstable and completely bound. Maybe she knew she was in bondage; perhaps the demons allowed her enough of her mind to realize she was trapped without hope.

How desperate her eyes must have looked to those who dared get close enough to see.

Jesus, in His righteousness, healed her because He saw what she would become, the devoted disciple who would faithfully stand by the cross as He took His last breath and one of the first to know of His resurrection. In His eyes, she was fully seen and loved despite her wretched situation.

Mary's incredible healing left her with one desire, a heart to serve Christ alone. She knew by grace alone she had been rescued from the demons that had plagued her mind.

A woman who has experienced great redemption will be sold out for the cause of Christ.

A woman who has experienced great redemption will be sold out for the cause of Christ.

She bent her life around being a follower of Christ. A woman who had nothing because of her brokenness had nothing to lose in becoming a disciple. She gave of her life as she ministered alongside the twelve. Their mission was clear - go, tell the gospel.

When Jesus spoke to the disciples and told them of His death to come, Mary was overcome because her heart didn't want to be without her Savior. In the middle of the chaos of the trial, she never wavered. She stood by the cross even after the other disciples fled, watching with horror as the blood dripped down His pale face mangled by the crown of thorns. She waited with Him until the end when the darkness came and the dirt below the cross pooled with red.

They lowered the body of her Savior from the cross, and she must have questioned, "How did it come to this? Why did He have to die?" Even as they placed His body in the grave, she stayed close. Mary's devotion proved unparalleled even at His death.

The silence among the disciples was devastating as each one dealt with their fears and betrayal. The ones who hid away from the gruesome crucifixion were left to ponder all that had taken place.

When the sun rose on the third day after Jesus' death, the warmth hit Mary's face as she opened her eyes. The sunrise was breathtaking as it rose across the hills of Jerusalem. As she came into the garden to anoint His body with spices, she saw the tomb's stone had been moved. Mary ran as fast as she could to the grave, dropping everything in her hands. When she looked inside the tomb, Jesus was gone, and only empty grave clothes remained. Panic overtook her as she wept violently, "They have taken the Lord out of the tomb, and we do not know where they have laid him" (John 20:2).

She ran back to the disciples as quickly as her feet would carry her. When Peter and John saw that His body was missing, they left and returned home, but not Mary. She stood at the door of the tomb and wept. Alone with her tears, Mary suddenly heard the voices of the angels. They longed to know why she was sobbing.

As she turned, a shadow cast in front of her. Her eyes were blurred with tears, and she could not make out the man as He spoke. "Woman, why are you crying? Whom do you seek?" As she shook with grief, the figure then spoke one word that suddenly made the tears in her eyes cease, and her heart quickened, "Mary." He spoke her name, and she knew, "Rabboni." She threw herself at His feet, weeping at the sight of the nail holes that marked Him. She reached for His hands to touch the holes made on her behalf. He said, "Do not cling to me, for I have not yet ascended to the Father; but go to my brothers and say to them, 'I am ascending to my Father and your Father, to my God and your God'" (John 20:17).

By grace, Mary was offered the first glimpse of her risen Savior. She saw He was alive again and He commissioned her to go and tell the others, "Jesus has risen!" She became the first to proclaim the Good News.

Just as quickly as she ran to tell of the missing body, Mary ran to tell the disciples the news. What honor was bestowed upon this woman who was privileged to be the first to see the Resurrection and the Life.

A Beautiful Story

From the beginning of Scripture to the end we are reminded that God writes a beautiful story. We see that He works all things together for our good and for His glory. Mary Magdalene was no exception. He worked things together for her good and for the benefit of the gospel. Mary may not have served God with the same devotion had she not been healed or plagued in the first place.

"And we know that for those who love God all things work together for good, for those who are called according to his purpose" (Romans 8:28).

My granny gave what she had as a sacrifice to Jesus. Her acts of love and devotion will be told as a memorial to her for generations to come. The testimony of a life well-lived is a witness to each of us in our daily reach for grand obedience. As we sit at desks writing books, serve in Sunday school classes, or rock little ones to sleep each night, our lives become a witness.

God isn't looking for grand. He is looking for our devotion.

God isn't looking for grand. He is looking for our devotion.

He sees the hidden mundane of our days and whispers, "I am here. Will you be devoted to me in this place?" Will we still be devoted when our faithfulness goes unseen by the world around us? When it is unnoticed by everyone but the people we physically touch with our hands? If there are no books written about our lives, or social media to display our actions, will we still act in obedience to Jesus who paid it all for us?

Mary Magdalene was a real Holy Mess, a life fully devoted to Christ in service and utter love. Faithfulness to Christ is what is required of a devoted life. God rewarded Mary's devotion, not with earthly things, but with heavenly reward. The act of hearing her name whispered in the garden would make the heart of anyone brought from death to life weep with great joy.

One day, when the doors of heaven open for me, what a sweet sound it will be as my name is whispered by Jesus. The One whose hands were pierced for me. The Savior whose head carried a crown of thorns for the benefit of our souls. The Healer who carried every ounce of our sin upon Him as He hung upon the cross.

My own life of devotion is a reflection of the healing He did in me.

As I wrote this chapter, I knew my granny's days were short. Her journey to heaven would soon come. As she held the pages of this book in her hands, a charge came from her frail voice, one I will carry with me all of my days, "Keep going, never give up, never stop writing or teaching, and never stop telling people about Jesus."

Devotion is the beautiful mark on a life sold out to the gospel alone.

I pray at the end of my days my family will say the same of me. That I will be known as a Holy Mess – a devoted, obedient daughter of God, and I pray when I get to heaven and see my Gran face to face again, I will be able to look her in the eye and tell her I kept the charge. Just like the marks on my granny's hands that show her devotion, the marks on our own lives testify to the same.

Our devotion to Jesus will be what drives us forward every day for the gospel.

We are devoted because His grace redeemed us from our mistakes, met us in the waiting, and healed us in our brokenness. He cleansed our sins, loved us in our rejection, and brought comfort to our grief. He reformed our desire for perfection, filled us with spiritual confidence, and transformed us completely. He hears us in prayer, faithfully blesses us in obedience, and lovingly calls us His Holy Mess.

Holy Mess Declaration

I declare, I will proclaim God's holiness over
my life as His beloved daughter.

I declare, He will reclaim my mistakes for His victories
and my waiting for His glorious purposes.

I declare, I will surrender the sin in my life
that has held me captive and allow Him to
heal the places in me that are desperately broken.

I declare, when grief comes like a flood over
my life I will rest in the power of His comfort.

When I am rejected, I will believe
the truth of who God says I am.

I declare, in the busyness of my days I will
rest at the Father's feet; I will give Him
the first and best of me always.

I declare, as God sanctifies my flesh and
spirit, I will surrender to the reckoning of God and the
transformation He desires to make in my life.

I declare I will take courage in God
who is my strength and shield.

I declare, as I walk with God in this life I will
do so in fervent prayer and faithful obedience.

I declare to the world I am the holy daughter
of the Most High God, saved by the blood of Christ.

And, I declare, no matter what mess comes
my way, He who redeems me is faithful,
and I will be His Holy Mess.

**(Get access to the online Bible study group, teaching videos and
more at www.holymessbook.com password WomenoftheBible)**

Acknowledgements

God put the idea for Holy Mess on my heart at a writer's conference three years ago. I feel like I have wrestled with God for every word but it has been worth every day and every tear. I have always heard that writers write what they know, and this is what I know, writers write what God makes them wrestle first.

There are so many people to thank for making Holy Mess come to life. Three years ago God put something in my heart and now you hold it in your hands. There are so many people in my life I owe a debt of gratitude for coming alongside of me in this journey.

First, I must thank and praise God for choosing a misfit like me, loving me, and using my life to the praise of His glory.

My husband, Jeremy, thank you for every meal cooked, basket of laundry folded, and hour you work to provide for our family so I can write words. Thank you for being willing to marry a girl like me, for showing me the love of Christ, and teaching me so many things I never knew about God.

My kids, thank you for letting mommy write, being patient and listening to me read and reread sentences to you.

Julie, thank you for believing in the calling God gave. Thank you for guarding my words as if they were your own and making me a better writer. I feel I owe you more than a thanks; this book would have never seen the light had it not been for you and that pencil.

Jessica, I don't know what would happen without Facetime. Thank you for the sacrifice of time and love you have given to this book and ministry. Team work makes the dream work.

My Mom, thank you for never giving up on me in the hard things.

My church families - Central Baptist and Jackson Park Baptist, thank you for loving me and my family through everything. Thank you for supporting Displaying Grace and Holy Mess. Thank you for giving me the space to teach and share the Gospel with women. I am forever grateful for you all.

Notes

Chapter 3 -

Warren W. Wiersbe, The Bible Exposition Commentary, Volume 1. (Colorado Springs: David C. Cook, 1989), 198

Herbert Lockyer, All the Women of the Bible. (Grand Rapids: Zondervan, 1967), 232

Chapter 7 -

Sarah Hagerty, Unseen. (Grand Rapids: Zondervan, 2017), 131

Oswald Chambers, My Utmost for His Highest. (Grand Rapids: Discovery House, 1992), 26

Chapter 10 -

"Spurgeon Quotes on Obedience," Girded with Truth: www.girdedwithtruth.org/spurgeon-quotes-on-obedience/ (2019)

Chapter 11 -

C. H. Spurgeon, and G. Holden Pike. Sermons of Rev. C. H. Spurgeon of London, Vol III. (New York; London: Funk & Wagnalls, 1892), 18-?

Scripture Index

Colossians 4:2

Chapter 10 -
Romans 8:29
John 8:36
Galatians 5:1
Judges 4:1
Romans 3:23
Romans 6:28
Romans 5:8
Romans 1:16

Romans 5:9
Romans 5:19
Romans 6:16
Judges 5:3
John 14:23-24

Chapter 11 -
Colossians 1:13-14
1 Corinthians
1:28-29
Hebrews 11:31

Galatians 2:20

Chapter 12 -
John 20:17
Romans 8:28

www.displayinggrace.com

Online Bible Study Group

Bible Study Live

Podcast

Blog

Bible Study Shop

Check out other titles from Michelle Rabon

Craving More:
21 Days to Cultivating the Habit of Being in God's Word

Seeking Him:
A Study of Psalm 119

Consumed Life:
A Woman's Guide to Studying God's Word

Made Alive:
A Study of Ephesians

Made in the USA
Columbia, SC
23 September 2021